BITTER ROOTS

FIVE GENERATIONS
OF A CHINESE FAMILY
IN AMERICA

BITTER ROOTS

FIVE GENERATIONS
OF A CHINESE FAMILY
IN AMERICA

BRUCE QUAN, JR.

Word by Word Press

Published by Word by Word Press
San Francisco, California

ISBN: 9798682626786

Titles: Perpetua Titling
Text: Times New Roman

Cover image: Lew Hing with daughter Rose and son Thomas Lew, c. 1899

DEDICATION

For my grandchildren:
May the dark clouds of racism
be dispersed in your lifetime.

This is the story of your family's odyssey from when your ancestors first arrived in America in the 1850s. It is also the story of our survival in the face of fierce anti-Chinese sentiment since the nineteenth century, as we continue to face the underlying racism pervasive in our own lives.

The symbol on the title page means "Family."

PREFACE

While completing this book, I took frequent breaks to read the contemporary news. In the May 5, 2020 Wall Street Journal, the front page headlines in the largest font on the page said: "Virus Widens Rift between U.S./China".

As I shelter in place, outside racism swirls around with anti-Asian incidents because the U.S. President has claimed the Coronavirus Pandemic started in China and that the Chinese are hiding the truth. Meanwhile, the President is also fanning the flames of racism by misusing the tragic death of George Floyd, a black man murdered by a Minneapolis policeman. The incident, captured on video, has led to thousands upon thousands of residents of cities large and small protesting the racism directed towards people of color by the whites in power for as long as the United States has existed. During that time, the whites made an example of my great-grandfather to teach the Chinese and other Asians to stay as second-class residents. It's been almost one hundred years since the white establishment brought down my great-grandfather at a time of tremendous racism. He's gone but the stain of racism remains.

Stephen Platt, American historian and writer, Professor of Chinese history at the University of Massachusetts Amherst, succinctly captured my own thinking:

> "Now, as then, the prospect of China becoming more like us has occasioned a collision between the American ideals and its fears—ideals of political stability and economic prosperity for China on the one hand and, on the other, fears that we will be undermined by a country whose people are willing to

work for wages far lower than our own (the exact same fears, it should be noted, that drove the original Chinese exclusion laws). America likes to think of itself as encouraging modernization, political liberalization, and economic development in China, but it is worth remembering that behind the outward charity of such impulses there has always lurked the companion fear that such changes, if they should prove too successful, might also prove our own undoing."

China is the only country of color which challenges the dominance of the Western white countries. As such, there will be uncase by the leaders and many whites towards those of Chinese descent, wherever they may be found. In America, racism and anti-Chinese sentiment will always be with my children, their children and beyond until an economic or military war settles the matter.

"It's Deja Vu all over again." (Thanks, Yogi Berra.)

Bruce Quan, Jr.
October 2020

A NOTE ABOUT THIS BOOK

This account of five generations of my family's life in America could simply be called an historical drama. The characters are all people who lived and breathed and walked the earth of China and California, from the 1850s to the present day. The hardships they endured, the successes they wrested from the tight-fisted grasp of the "White Devils" whose racism shaped and distorted their lives and mine—all are true although at times harsh and almost unbelievable. But we persisted, and built a legacy of hard work, self-determination, dignity, worth and family strength.

As the reader will see, I have constructed and dramatized many conversations and meetings that "most likely" took place among my ancestors and the people they lived and worked with—I have italicized these exchanges and events in the hope that these are recognized clearly as fictional, but nonetheless based on facts and events that I know occurred for my family.

Although this drama may be of great interest to my widespread and far-flung family, it is my hope and intention that these fact-based stories will enlighten, encourage and inspire whoever reads them—students, historians, Asian-Americans and all other peoples of different races who may recognize themselves or their families in this drama—in short, we human beings who inhabit our world with skins of different shades, and languages made of different sounds, but with minds and hearts aligned to what is good and true in life, taught to us by our mothers and fathers, aunties and uncles, brothers and sisters and family friends, down through the generations.

TABLE OF CONTENTS

PART ONE

THE RISE AND FALL OF THE FIRST CHINESE INDUSTRIALIST IN AMERICA

CHAPTER ONE — OBITUARY

Obituary of Lew Hing – 1934 1

CHAPTER TWO — THE BEGINNING

American Duplicity – 1868 4
Lew Hing Leaves Hong Kong – 1869 8
Into the Maelstrom of Misery – 1870s – 1890s 13
Arriving in San Francisco – 1869 17
The Golden Spike – 1869 22
Introduction to Chinatown 25
Hing Kee & Co 29
Missionary School 30
Beginning a Friendship – 1871 33
Fate Intervenes – 1872 35

CHAPTER THREE — THE YEARS OF GROWTH 1872 - 1903

Accepting New Responsibilities – 1872 39
1876 Smallpox Epidemic 45
A Learning Experience 48
U.S. Congress Passes Page Act Limiting Entry of Chinese Women – 1875 51
Lew Hing Married In Absentia – 1877 52
Chin Shee Successfully Arrives in the United States – 1877 53
Anti-Chinese Riot in San Francisco – 1877 55

China Establishes a Consulate in San Francisco – 1878 58
California Leaders Attempt to Limit Impact of Chinese on its Economy – 1870s – 1880s.......... 59
The United States Congress Passes the 1882 Chinese Exclusion Act.......... 63
Exclusion Act Affects Lew Hing – 1883.......... 65
Launching a New Venture: Pacific Fruit Packing Company – 1883-1888.......... 72
Pacific Fruit Packing Company Opens for Business – 1888.......... 76
Congress Passes Geary Act Extending Exclusion of Chinese – 1892.......... 78
Whites Target Pacific Fruit Packing Company – 1891-1893.......... 80
Social Unrest Threatens Stability in Chinatown – 1895 83
A Calculated Marriage – 1898.......... 86
White Canners' Combine Threatens Existence of Pacific Fruit Packers Company – 1899.......... 88
The Plague Threat – 1900.......... 91
White Competition Drives Lew Hing Out of the Cannery Business – 1902.......... 96
The Reality of China Hits Home – 1902-1903.......... 98

CHAPTER FOUR ~ RETURN TO AMERICA 1903 - 1906

Planning a New Cannery in Oakland – 1903.......... 101
Separating Business from Family.......... 108
The Crown Jewel of His Empire – 1904.......... 113

CHAPTER FIVE ~ MAJOR BUSINESS SUCCESS

The Great San Francisco Earthquake – 1906....... 117
A Kinsman to the Rescue.............................. 119
The White Devil's Lies.................................. 124
City Fathers Say No to Chinatown – 1906.......... 129
Direct Family Control of Underground Activities – 1906 134
"Chinatown, My Chinatown" – 1908................. 140
Establishing the Canton Bank – 1908................ 148
Chinatown Re-Opens – 1908-1910................. 150

CHAPTER SIX ~ TRUSTED LIEUTENANTS

Daughter Yuet Yung and Son-in-Law Quan Yeen......151

CHAPTER SEVEN ~ U.S. ATTITUDE TOWARDS CHINA

Chinese Revolution and American Attitudes Towards Chinese – 1908-1912.............. 158
A Greater Presence in Chinatown – 1906-1915.... 166
A Beneficial Relationship – 1903-1923.............. 167
Alien Land Laws – 1913................................ 170
Lew Hing Invests in Mexico: Chinese-Mexican Mercantile Company – 1913................. 172
The Panama Canal and the Panama Pacific International Exposition –1915............... 176
A Boost to the Bottom Line – 1914-1918........... 182
China Mail Steamship Lines – 1915.................. 184
The Pancho Villa Episode.............................. 187
The Pershing Chinese Story............................ 190
Hoover Redux.. 192

CHAPTER EIGHT ~ THE FALL
1923 – 1926

Fickle Winds of Fate.. 194
China Mail Steamship Lines Forced into
Bankruptcy—1923................................ 198
Conspiracy to Close Ethnic Banks..................... 201
Canton Bank on the Watch List......................... 208
Canton Bank in Trouble – 1923......................... 210
Death Knell for Canton Bank............................ 215
The Crown Jewel Loses its Luster..................... 219

CHAPTER NINE ~ GONE AND FORGOTTEN
1926 – 1934

Lew Hing and James Rolph................................ 225
An Attempt to Rise Back Up.............................. 226

~ PART TWO ~

CHINATOWN AS SANCTUARY 1930S TO 1960S

Racism Alive and Well in America—1930s............. 231
Existing in the Confines of Chinatown – 1934......... 232
A Life Altered by Racial Prejudice – 1940-1965....... 236
Racial Prejudice in the Service – 1942.................. 238
The Incident in New Orleans While at Officer
Candidate School 1945.......................... 239
Dreams and Ambitions Thwarted – 1946............... 241
Racism on Full Display – 1952........................... 242
Legacy of Hate – 1953.................................... 245
In the Belly of the Beast – 1958.......................... 247
Segregated Schools – 1958-1964........................ 249
Racism in the Open – Fall 1964.......................... 251

ஃ PART THREE ஃ

UNDERCURRENTS OF RACISM REMAIN

Civil Rights Movement – 1965 255
Responding to Racism – 1975 256
Racism in Practice – 1978-1984 259
Racial Profiling is Alive and Well – 1989 261
Coronavirus: What Attacks on Asians Reveal about American Identity – 2020 265

POSTSCRIPT 267

FAMILY GALLERY 271

APPENDIX A: LIST OF LEW HING BUSINESSES AND INVESTMENTS 278

APPENDIX B: FAMILY GENEALOGY CHARTS 280

ABOUT THE AUTHOR 283

PART ONE

THE RISE AND FALL OF THE FIRST CHINESE INDUSTRIALIST IN AMERICA

ONE

OBITUARY

From the Oakland Tribune, 1934

NOTED CHINESE ROMANTIC LIFE COMES TO END

Immigrant Boy Who Rose to
High Position in Industry
Dies Peacefully at Home

Lew Hing, Chinese immigrant boy who became an American captain of industry was dead today at his home, 3750 Lakeshore Avenue, aged 77.

He died peacefully, surrounded by his wife and his three sons instead of violently at the hands of a compatriot gunman, as he had at one time feared. Behind him Lew Hing left a record of business success from a humble beginning that reads like a collaboration of Pearl Buck and Horatio Alger. He came to California from his native China in 1868, in the days when immigrants were not required to show that they were capable of self support, and in the entire family of the 11-year-old boy who spoke no English there was not enough money to provide rice for more than a few days ahead.

STARTED IN CANNERY

Lew went to work in a can factory and after a few years of hard manual labor, began to rise. In a few years more he owned the cannery. Later he established the Pacific Coast Canning Co., which has a large plant in West Oakland, and became its president. Then he became president of the Canton Bank in San Francisco, vice-president and general manager of the China Mail Steamship Co.

By this time his operations were international and he now organized the Chinese-Mexican Mercantile Company of Mexicali. He became a leading figure in the local import trade with the establishment of the Hop Wo Lung Merchandise Co. of San Francisco of which he was president, and then founded the Sing Chong Company on Grant Avenue, San Francisco, to care for the retail end.

HEADED HATE LIST

In 1918 he led a movement to increase the capitalization of the China Mail Company from $2,500,000 to $10,000,000, a course which was violently opposed by many of the ultra-conservative stockholders. Secret meetings were held in Chinatown alleys, and a "hate list" was prepared with Lew's name at the head of it. The list fell into the hands of the police and there were immediately placed constant guards over all those named on it. For months, whenever Lew walked in Oakland or San Francisco, armed men sauntered unobtrusively at a little distance, watching for any attempt to attack him.

DIRECTOR KILLED

Their need for their care was shown when Fong Wing, a director of the company and one whose name followed Lew's on the "hate list" grew careless after several months and stepped out of his door in San Francisco's Chinatown without waiting for his escort. A bullet fired from ambush killed him almost as he set foot in the street. Finally the feeling died down and Lew walked again in safety.

Within the past few years he has been retiring from one after another of his enterprises and turning as many of his affairs as possible over to his sons-Lew Gow, Thomas Lew and Ralph Lew. Besides his wife and three sons, Lew is survived by four daughters: Mrs. Quan Yuan, Mrs. C.W. Ho, Mrs. Ng Ming Hing and Mrs. F.S Moon. His funeral which will be strictly occidental, will be held Tuesday at noon at the Chinese Presbyterian Church, Eighth and Alice Streets, with interment in Mountain View Cemetery.

During his lifetime, 1858 -1934, Lew Hing belonged to an ethnic group described by whites as "Sneaky Oriental", "Yellow Peril", "Chinese menace", "indispensable enemy" and their Chinatown as a "filthy nest of iniquity and rottenness"; the Chinese were considered an inferior race unassimilable to the American nation. Succeeding in spite of white animus towards Chinese during his life and for which he may have paid dearly for daring to be successful, Lew Hing's journey through life was extraordinary.

TWO

THE BEGINNING

AMERICAN DUPLICITY 1868

Driven by the need for workers to help construct the Transcontinental Railroad, America came to the bargaining table with China and the result was the 1868 Burlingame Treaty. This international agreement secured U.S. access to Chinese workers by guaranteeing rights of free migration to both Chinese and Americans.

Intending to solidify the connection between the eastern and western halves of the United States, the U.S. Congress authorized construction of the Transcontinental Railroad during the upheavals of the Civil War in 1862. With the north and south at war, there were labor shortages which delayed the project for years. At war's end, Central Pacific Railroad began recruiting Chinese workers, eventually in numbers reaching well over ten thousand at a time. The U.S. government sought to secure access to Chinese workers, many of whom worked on three-year contracts, despite Chinese laws banning emigration by Chinese. The Burlingame Treaty was the first international agreement signed since the Opium War (1839-42) that dealt with Chinese on equal terms and secured the rights of Chinese to free immigration and travel within the United States and the most favored nation status in trade.

Signed in Washington on July 28, 1868 supplementing the June 18, 1858 Tientsin Treaty and effective on November 23, 1869, Article V of the treaty provided:

> "The United States of America and the Emperor of China cordially recognize the inherent and inalienable right of man to change his home and allegiance, and also the mutual advantage of the free migration and emigration of their citizens and subjects respectively from one country to the other, for purposes of curiosity, of trade, or as permanent residents. The high contracting parties, therefore, join in reprobating any other than an entirely voluntary emigration for these purposes. They consequently agree to pass laws making it a penal offence for a citizen of the United States or Chinese subjects to take Chinese subjects either to the United States or to any other foreign country, or for a Chinese subject or citizen of the United States to take citizens of the United States to China or to any other foreign country, without their free and voluntary consent respectively."

The Burlingame Treaty intended to permit almost unlimited and unrestricted immigration by Chinese to the United States. It annulled several state laws that had restricted Chinese immigration. Passed at a time when significant domestic opposition to Chinese immigration was emerging, it was the final agreement with China that encouraged immigration before the federal government, urged on by racist state and local officials in California, introduced severe restrictions.

China was concerned with protecting its subjects who had immigrated and continued to immigrate. Since the discovery of gold in 1849, Chinese had come to California in substantial numbers. Chased out of the gold fields by discriminatory laws of California, they were desperate to survive and soon were taken advantage of by white businesses. Their numbers gradually increased during the mid-nineteenth century. By the mid 1860s, approximately 50,000 Chinese lived in California alone.

China also wanted recognition of its own territorial integrity and national sovereignty. Similar to agreements with other national powers, the agreement permitted China to have consuls at American ports.

Bottom line, the United States' entry into the agreement was mainly economic—more access for its people and products to the Chinese market, while China's goal was political—recognition and protection for its subjects seeking to immigrate.

The United States had no intention of honoring its words set forth in the Burlingame Treaty and the main reason was the anti-Chinese sentiment in California.

When gold was discovered at Sutter's Mill, white California was not a particularly welcoming place for new arrivals from Mexico and other parts of Central and South America. Experienced foreign miners who knew how to extract the gold from streams and hillsides were rewarded by white California politicians who imposed a state tax on foreign miners and subjected them to episodes of violence and mistreatment.

However, white California reserved the worst in treatment for the Chinese. The early Chinese were subjected to continual hostility, excluded from all but the poorest, worked-over and exhausted mining claims.

While the origin of the phrase "Chinaman's chance" is not well documented and often attributable to the dangerous work of Chinese railroad workers in the 1860s, it was frequently used as a pejorative and has been used from the 1860s to the present towards Chinese.

Animus towards the Chinese increased from those early years and soon became institutionalized. Charles J. McClain, professor at Berkeley Law and noted scholar in this field, opined:

> "In short, the Chinese worked too hard (often for less pay than others were willing to accept), saved too much, and spent too little. In addition, they looked and behaved differently from the majority population. Beneath all the surface rationalizations, this was to be the gravamen of the complaint against the Chinese through the many phases of the anti-Chinese movement in California."[1]

The anti-Chinese movement led to a series of state and local laws meant to force the Chinese to leave California or to make it extremely difficult or expensive for them to stay.

For example, the California legislature enacted a variety of fees and taxes on arriving Chinese immigrants, then a tax of $2.50 a month on most Chinese residents. They were forbidden to live in certain parts of cities, not allowed in hospitals, never able to gain citizenship unless born in America,

---

[1] McClain, Charles J., *In Search of Equality: The Chinese Struggle against Discrimination in Nineteenth-Century America*, University of California Press. 1994. p 10

and not allowed to testify in court or vote. Chinese children were excluded from the state's public schools.

At the local level, the San Francisco Board of Supervisors joined in discriminating against the Chinese with such laws as banning peddlers (targeting Chinese) from the common practice of carrying goods on poles, to directly targeting Chinese laundries by imposing punitive fees and the cubic air law regulating the size of rooms in lodging-houses, an attempt to limit the number of rooms which could house Chinese in the restricted twelve square blocks in Chinatown.

As the anti-Chinese sentiment spread from California throughout the United States, with the natural proclivity of the whites to revert to their base instincts of racial prejudice when they do not like results, it was impossible for America to adhere to the intent of the Burlingame Treaty.

The Chinese fought back in the late 1860s and early 1870s, waging long and ultimately successful campaigns such as winning the right to testify in court and to end enforcement of the discriminatory tax on foreign miners, further outraging the white Californians.

In the end, the white politicians in California put an end to this tug of war over equal rights. They championed and convinced the rest of the white politicians in Congress to pass the 1875 Page Act and 1882 Chinese Exclusion Act, the first of several laws specifically targeting one ethnic group, the Chinese, for exclusion.

LEW HING LEAVES HONG KONG

1869

Under the control of the British since 1841 as part of the spoils of the Opium War, the ban on emigration by China of its subjects didn't apply to Hong Kong where Lew Hing, a young boy of eleven was spending his last day at school.

The dim light of the gas lamp illuminated the dormitory room where the students were spending their last night. Earlier, they laughed and joked, packing their meager belongings; for each, the cheerfulness masked anxiety and dread of what lay ahead. China was still in the throes of famine, drought, war and corruption. Civil unrest dominated the landscape of Southern China. Here, students all came from there, whether from the rival Sze Yup or Sam Yup districts of Guangdong Province There was no rivalry or animosity because of where they were from. Here, they were at least safe, despite the second-class citizenship status under British rule. Lew Hing slept uncomfortably, tossing and turning until the morning light.

The next day, the parents or guardians would arrive to take the boys home or to the next place where they would apprentice. Arriving the next morning, His father, Lew Nai Rong, and mother, Mei Shi Shee, went to the office to settle accounts and then to the classroom to meet with his teacher who reported:

"Lew Hing has acquitted himself very well. He is not afraid of taking the lead and is a creative problem solver. Very bright and a quick study when he puts his mind to it, he is also high spirited, curious and adventurous; likely to get into trouble. For example, he was told to stay out of the white part of town but kept sneaking back in only to be chased out by the police on several occasions. Even when they told him to stay away or they would teach him a lesson, he would return time and again."

Having the undivided attention of his parents was unusual and Lew Hing was at first hesitant to express himself. The few days they spent exploring Hong Kong in a relaxed manner allowed him to relax and for the first time, he enjoyed their company without reservation.

Sitting with his parents at the table next to the window the morning of his departure, his baggage next to him, sipping tea and eating porridge, he gazed wistfully at his parents. Not having seen his mother and father since his father brought him to Hong Kong and remembering the tearful goodbye with his mother, he studied their faces and thought to himself, *"I remember them being youthful but now they seemed so much older; the strain of age and the vicissitudes of living among the turmoil in China mirrored in their faces."*

Hong Kong Harbor, c. 1869

The cloudless pale blue skies of the morning reminded Lew Hing of the time he arrived in Hong Kong six years ago. He remembered his father accompanying him on the long journey from Canton to attend school, the anxiety burdening him when his father left, and how long it took for him to adjust to his new surroundings. Those feelings surfaced again as he contemplated joining his brother in America.

As he reflected on the upcoming journey, he unconsciously touched his pocket, which held the letter from his father. It told him he would not be returning to Canton, but would go to America to join his older brother who had started a dry goods store, Hing Kee & Co.

His mother did her best to cheer him up, telling him of the riches in America and how well his older brother was doing, sending money back to help the family through the tough times now in China.

"You are now an adult and must accept responsibility to help care for the family. We will miss you but know that with your older brother, you will be safe and learn to do business so when you marry, you will be able to provide for your family."

His father then spoke. *"First, to travel so far across the ocean is not easy and I wish there was a fellow clansman to travel with you. Because you are Chinese and not a wealthy merchant, the whites will only allow you to stay below deck in a space crowded with others. You must carefully wrap your money in this special body wrap your mother has made for you,"* he said as he handed over the cloth wrap. *"If you find yourself in trouble, seek out someone to be your friend and if that friend protects you, give him some money in gratitude for his kindness."*

His father made sure Lew Hing nodded his understanding. *"You must also protect the dried meat and preserved plums and fruit in pouches your mother has sewn inside the back of your coat. The white devil's food is nearly inedible. Always find a place to sleep with your back to a wall."*

Lew Hing listened carefully but was frightened by what his father then said, *"I know about how perilous the journey is as I experienced it in the 1850s before you were born. The whites running the ship didn't care about us. When some died during the journey, they just threw the dead bodies and their baggage overboard without a second thought. They were cruel and otherwise condescending, calling us cock-roaches."*

His father then sipped tea before continuing. *"It was a relief when we finally reached "Gold Mountain." Most of us were in a hurry to get to the gold country but once I got there, the whites were even more cruel towards Chinese. They robbed and murdered those lucky enough to find gold. We were not allowed to register good claims but only ones that had been exhausted. In addition, we were required to pay a tax which the whites didn't have to pay. We always were wary around the whites as I saw them once, drunk with guns, taking two countrymen from our camp, march them to a low-lying branch, tie them together by their queues, drape them over the branch and while they dangled, shot them dead for fun. We always ran away when they came looking for us. I left after only one week, scared for my life."*

His father paused, ate some porridge and continued. *"Returning to San Francisco, I looked for work but the only work available was as a conscripted laborer. The whites around us near the wharves next to Chinatown were as vile and decadent as those in the gold country; whites were always drunk, fighting and filthy and smelly from not having washed for days, perhaps weeks! They made no secret of hating us and for that reason, we found refuge and safety in Chinatown.*

"But Chinatown was so crowded and the only place to sleep was in dark and smelly basements where we shared space with rats and cockroaches. I couldn't stand it so I camped along the shores of the bay until my money almost ran out. I had just enough money to buy a ticket back home. You are lucky, you have someone waiting for you with decent food and a place to sleep. According to your brother, life for Chinese in California is much better now, the whites are not

so full of hate for us, so I am confident a good future lies ahead for you."

Finally, his father, remembering what Lew Hing's teacher had said, admonished him.

"Be careful, when dealing with the white man, look down, wait for them to speak first and only answer yes or no. You are considered different from them, like a dog on two legs. You have no rights. They can rob you or kill you for looking at them the wrong way and nothing will happen to them."

Lew Hing thought about begging his parents to let him go back with them to Canton but knew there, he would just be another mouth to feed without hope of helping the family. He only sighed and slowly picked up his baggage and followed his parents out of the restaurant.

They made their way to the dock where the three-masted steamship was tied up. He turned to say goodbye and his mother held him tightly against her breast and tearfully whispered words of encouragement. His father stood by and both of them nodded goodbye as his father said, *"May the Gods look favorably upon you."* With that, Lew Hing turned and walked out of their lives, not knowing if he would ever see them again.

INTO THE MAELSTROM OF MISERY

1870s - 1890s

The 1870s-1890s were an intense period of anti-Chinese sentiment and violence throughout the United States. The anti-Chinese agitation drove Chinese from many settlements in rural California to San Francisco, creating crowded conditions and more problems. As the depression deepened in the

United States, in California and the West, crowds of unemployed white laborers began to persecute the Chinese, who they claimed were taking their places in the labor force.

San Francisco, c. 1865

In California and cities in California, white politicians responded favorably to the agitation with legislation discriminating against the Chinese, prompting the Chinese to respond by hiring white attorneys to challenge the laws, many of which were ultimately ruled unconstitutional by state and federal Supreme Courts.

Contrary to the mysterious Chinatown often portrayed among the whites, Chinatown was really a prison where the police knew every activity which transpired there. In San Francisco, the police were omnipresent and the Chinese under constant surveillance.

From the 1870s to the early decades of the 20th century, as researched by historian Barbara Berlund, not only did the whites literally invade the living spaces of the Chinese, but they also created impressions from their visits of an unassimilable race—ungodly, filthy and vice-ridden. Here is an excerpt from Berlund's book that describes it well:

> White visitors' use of police guides added another level of surveillance to the police presence in the area. Tourists, after all, often chose police guides not just because of safety concerns but also for the knowledge and access to Chinatown they could provide—a by-product....
>
> Police guides, moreover, were known for deploying quite brutal, invasive, and generally disrespectful tactics that included kicking doors open, forcing their way into private living quarters, waking people from sleep, and shining bright lights into people's faces. Whether these encounters were staged or not, they made violence an expected part of the tourist experience in Chinatown.
>
> Visitors would then go away and write up their impressions of the Chinese in America, giving as historical facts their impressions based on these guided tours.
>
> In the tourist literature, Chinese restaurants were portrayed as violating norms of public health as well as various food taboos; opium dens were used to conjure images of Chinese as particularly prone to vice; joss houses were described in ways that emphasized unassimilability and difference in the form of heathenism; and theaters were employed to illuminate issues about Chinese Laborers and the backwardness of Chinese culture.
>
> The overall picture fortified the image of Chinese immigrants as utterly alien, insurmountably different, and from a culture that was considerably

> less evolutionarily elevated than that found in nineteenth-century America. The themes of unassimilability, contamination, labor competition, and vice were nodes around which the nineteenth-century image of 'the Oriental' was structured in the dominant culture's imagination. Rather than constructing completely novel images of Chinese immigrants, tourist literature mobilized and elaborated upon themes already in circulation. In the decades prior to the gold rush, the Chinese immigrants who had come to the United States settled mainly on the Eastern seaboard and were generally viewed as exotic curiosities. The unprecedented numbers of Chinese immigrants that arrived in San Francisco prior to the Exclusion Act, however, could not be understood through definitions that linked differences with notions of visitors from a distant, far away land. Instead, they necessitated a more direct subordination through cultural ordering that positioned Chinese immigrants within the nation's operative racial hierarchies and was informed by representation of 'the Oriental' as a permanent, threatening, and alien presence."[2]

One chronicler of the Chinatown tourist experience, Reverend Otis Gibson, decried these methods of studying the "Chinese Question." He even turned devil's advocate with the white readers:

> "Suppose the tables turned," he wrote, "and curious Chinamen escorted by some 'kind and intelligent

---

[2] Berlund, Barbara. *Making San Francisco American: Cultural Frontiers in the Urban West, 1846-1906*, University Press of Kansas: Lawrence KS 2007. Ch. 3 "Making Race in the City: Chinatown's Tourist Terrain"

> policeman' should make a raid upon American bedrooms, about twelve or one o'clock at night, solely for the delectation of the Chinamen, and so that some Chinese correspondent could write sensational letters to the Pekin Gazette. "How," [Gibson asked] "would the shoe fit on that foot? One might as well write up 'The Americans as They Are' from a visit to the Five Points in New York."[3]

Lew Hing, a young boy of eleven, was about to enter a strange and forbidding place.

ARRIVING IN SAN FRANCISCO
1869

Those first days of the voyage, he was like a rabbit caught in the sights of a hunter. Several of the men, all dressed in identical uniforms, eyed him carefully, knowing he must have money and food on his person.

Lew Hing was nervous, trying to remember the advice of his father to find a place against the wall to sleep. He cast his eyes about the steerage area but saw no eye contact or a smile in return. Was he to be as a lamb, waiting to be slaughtered and then thrown overboard? Who would miss him?

Too nervous to close his eyes and welcome sleep, he began to feel disoriented. So he took to staying on the deck in the evenings when he was most vulnerable, hoping that his cries could be heard by the crew if he was accosted.

There, cold winds swirled around like a spinning top, enveloping him in the darkness of the night air, the pungent sea air filling his nostrils as he huddled against the bulkhead

---

[3] Gibson, Otis, *Chinese in America,* (Cincinnati: Hitchcock and Walden, 1877), pp. 93-94.

fending off the chill. Concentrating on the rhythmic sound of the waves lapping against the hull, he tried to ease the passing of time until the morning light.

At dawn, there was an exodus of people from below, rushing out like lemmings to claim the best spots on the deck, streaming out to purge the bad air from their lungs, hoping the sun might purge the bad odors from their bodies.

Lew Hing, like a fish swimming upstream against the multitude swimming downstream, pushed his way through to reenter steerage. Surrounded by abandoned blankets and clothing in the dank, dark, stinking compartment, he surveyed the mess left behind. Those early days caused him to curse and wonder if he would survive. The challenges came when he was exhausted from staying on deck and he had to find a place to sleep. Several days into the voyage, no sooner had he nodded off when he heard a voice above him. Opening his eyes, he saw an older boy standing over him.

"Give me your money. I know you have money," he said as he leaned down and tried to pull the coat off Lew Hing. Fighting back with all his might and but nearly exhausted, he bit the boy in the arm so hard that he let go of the jacket, backing off, glaring. The next day, the same boy tried again, but this time, a well-built, taller, older man came to his defense.

"Who are you?" Lew Hing asked warily.

"I am Ah Chew and I have a son your age in my village. Because of the drought and bandits, I could not find work back home so I am going to America as conscripted labor to work."

"What do you mean 'conscripted labor'?" Lew Hing responded, puzzled.

"I signed an agreement to go to America to guaranteed work. The labor contractor pays my way to America so I am indebted to him and must pay him back from my wages."

Lew Hing thought to himself upon hearing the answer. "Now I know why father refused that kind of work. It's really being an indentured worker; one with no rights."

The older man was grateful to be able to find someone who was as educated as Lew Hing was. *"My father sent me to Canton for education and when I returned, our village and farms were destroyed. I hope to work in America for three years, save enough money and return back home with enough money to start a business with my clansmen in the village.*

Lew Hing responded, "My brother is already in San Francisco. He started a business and has enough business to send for me to come and help. I'm lucky to have made friends with you as my father worried that the most dangerous part of my journey would be traveling on the ship alone."

Having someone to speak with helped pass the time and gradually, Lew Hing accepted Ah Chew's help, from acting as his protector as he slept and while he was in line for food. In the early days of the voyage, when he was in the food line, older boys elbowed him aside and when he was able to get food, they took it away from him. He would then eat some of what his mother had packed for him in the pouches to ward off hunger. Fortunately, Ah Chew's presence stopped that.

As the ship from Hong Kong slowly entered San Francisco Bay, the blasts of the ship's horn alerted the passengers to the pending arrival. The Chinese rushed out, lining the rails for the first look at their chance for a spin at the wheel of fortune. All through the voyage, they occupied their time by telling what they would do with their riches if they struck gold.

"Gold Mountain!" some murmured as few waved their hands in joyful gestures. As the gangplank lowered, the crowds pushed forward, as if they were fleeing a sinking ship.

San Francisco Waterfront, c. 1860s

They were stopped by the burly white crewmen who had placed ropes from the first-class entrance to the gangway, creating a wide path for the white passengers and Chinese merchants who traveled first class to exit first.

As the Sam Yup Chinese merchants passed, speaking out loud and looking at the Sze Yup laborers with disdain, their look did not escape Lew Hing's eyes. He thought to himself, *we are all Chinese so why do you despise us? Is it because we speak different dialects?*

At the dock, the labor contractor sat at a table while two assistants stood by the gangplank directing those men who wore clothes identifying them to the table.

White hoodlums, mostly teenage boys, stood at a distance, shouting epithets and hurling insults at the laborers and threatening to do them harm.

At the top of the gangplank, Lew Hing and Ah Chew were nearly the last to depart. Lew Hing motioned to Ah Chew to a spot where they were alone.

"Thank you for being my friend on the voyage. The Gods smiled on me." He then reached into his pocket and withdrew some money, pressed it into the hand of a surprised Ah Chew who initially refused.

"My reward is finding someone to pass the time with across the ocean. There is no need to pay me."

Lew Hing responded, *"It was my father's wish that if the Gods chose to protect me, I must honor their choice."*

With that gesture, Lew Hing and Ah Chew bowed to each other and made their way to their future.

Leaving the ship with a brief glance back and the exaltation of having survived the voyage, Lew Hing surveyed San Francisco. There were more white people than he had ever seen and he thought to himself, *"It is the reverse of Hong Kong; here we are in the minority and they are in the majority. He said the whites, like in Hong Kong, don't like us. I must be careful as there are too many whites."*

He observed a group of Chinese walking up the hill and hurried to walk with them for protection. As they approached a park he saw fewer whites and more Chinese. He breathed a sigh of relief to be among his own kind but surprised at how run-down and crowded it was compared to the areas he observed on his walk.

His first thought was to find a place with real food, not lukewarm soup, black bread, boiled potatoes, herring and stringy meat. With the address of his brother's shop in his pocket and hunger pulling at his stomach, he stopped at a small restaurant, attracted by the smell of food he was familiar with but had not tasted for more than a month.

THE GOLDEN SPIKE

1869

Lew Hing arrived in San Francisco a couple of months after America had celebrated a momentous occasion—the joining of the eastern and western parts of America by the transcontinental railroad. Instead of taking six months to sail from the east coast around the Horn to the west coast, or traveling overland by wagon—both fraught with unknown risks—now travel would be much easier and take much less time.

Transcontinental Railroad "Golden Spike" Ceremony, 1869

This project had long been contemplated when President Abraham Lincoln, in the midst of the Civil War, signed the Pacific Railroad Act into law in 1862. Two railroads, Central Pacific and Union Pacific, were granted the right to build the railroad. Central Pacific's mandate was to construct the rails eastward from Sacramento. Little progress was made in the early years due to the war. When construction began in earnest in 1865, white workers left quickly due to the difficulty of labor.

Desperate, Charles Crocker, in charge of construction for the Central Pacific, began hiring Chinese laborers. Despite being considered by whites to be an inferior race, the Chinese proved to be tireless workers and Crocker hired more of them; some 11,000 were toiling under brutal working conditions in the Sierra Nevada by early 1867. By early 1869, Central Pacific and Union Pacific were headed to Salt Lake City, cutting many corners (including building shoddy bridges or sections of track that would have to be rebuilt later) in their race to get ahead.

By early 1869, the companies were working only miles from each other, and in March the newly inaugurated President Ulysses S. Grant announced he would withhold federal aid until the two railroad companies agreed on a meeting point. They decided on Promontory Summit, north of the Great Salt Lake, some 690 track miles from Sacramento and 1,086 from Omaha.

On May 10, after several delays, a crowd of workers and dignitaries watched as the final spike was driven linking the Central Pacific and the Union Pacific in the "Golden Spike Ceremony." No Chinese were allowed to be in the picture memorializing the event despite their blood, sweat and tears in helping build the railroad.

The contributions of the Chinese were never acknowledged at subsequent celebrations of the landmark event until the 150th celebration in 2019, perhaps because it was hard to ignore that the Secretary of Transportation was a Chinese-American woman.

Chinese attend 150th Anniversary of the Golden Spike, 2019

Among the best railroad builders in the world, the Chinese could lay ten miles of track in one day, and through their efforts, the transcontinental railroad was completed seven years ahead of schedule. For three years, they built tracks through the solid granite of the Sierra Nevada Mountains. They built track through snow piled stories high. They climbed out of avalanches, leaving the dead beneath the snow. They fought off Irish workers. Some even struck for better pay and improved working conditions. When the Central Pacific rail executive Charles Crocker cut off their food supply and threatened to replace them, it was he who gave in; they won a two dollars a day raise.

All in all, about 1,200 of the 11,000 Chinese workers on the Central Pacific were killed by the elements, by sickness, and by dynamite blasts. Despite and because of their heroics, the remaining Chinese American railroad workers lost their jobs, with workers dispersing throughout the country looking for work. Thousands eventually returned to California over the following months.

One of those who came back to San Francisco was Lew Yu-tang, from the District of Sun-Ning, village of Liao.

INTRODUCTION TO CHINATOWN

An exhausted Lew Yu-tang straggled into San Francisco the same day the ship on which Lew Hing was a passenger arrived at the dock. Hungry, he headed to Chinatown looking to eat real food. He had traveled for nearly as long as a ship's voyage from Hong Kong to San Francisco, but overland from Utah to San Francisco was infinitely more exhausting. Approaching Chinatown and smelling the familiar aroma of Chinese food, he thought back to the day he left Promontory Point, Utah in 1869. The ceremony uniting the east and the west concluded, the white owners kicked out the Chinese workers.

"Aieeyah, where do we go now that the railroad is built?" Chew, a fellow railroad worker bemoaned to the Chinese laborers huddled around the glowing embers of the fire as the chilly air enveloped them.

"I'm off to Marysville where some clansmen from my district back home are living. They say there is still gold to be found," Fong chimed in.

"Me, I'm going to Arizona, that's where my clansmen are located; they'll help me out," Owyang spoke.

"I'm going to take my chances and look for work in San Francisco. Hopefully, I'll have enough for one decent meal, a woman, gambling and opium!" Lew joked.

Next day, they packed their meager belongings, slid a pole through the tied bundles, bid farewell to each other and left to find their fate.

"Hey you, Chinaman, you aren't allowed on the train," yelled the white conductor as Lew attempted to board.

"I helped build this railroad," Lew said in broken English. "I should be able to ride it."

"Get off before I throw you off! No stinking heathens are allowed to sit with decent white folks" the conductor said. "If you want to get to San Francisco, use a mule," the conductor said laughingly.

Weeks later, arriving in San Francisco, he found a restaurant and sat at the only available table across from a young boy who looked up warily as Lew Yu, dusty and disheveled, sat down after dusting himself off. Looking at the

San Francisco Chinatown, c. 1860s

bowl of rice porridge the boy was eating, he ordered the same, cheap but filling.

Waiting for his food, Lew Yu glanced around the restaurant, wondering if the others there were his competition for the scarce jobs only available to those like him. He remembered the taunting of the white foreman of the railroad crew who called Chinese celestials, *"Celestials are like dogs because they will do anything, even the hardest, most dangerous and dirty work and work like dogs for almost nothing."*

"Excuse me and my appearance. My name is Lew Yu," he said to the boy. "I've traveled a long way from my last job laying tracks for a railroad. It took me weeks to reach here as the Lo Faan (white devil) wouldn't let me ride the train."

The boy only nodded, gesturing no opposition.

Lew Yu sized up the boy and continued speaking, *"I came from China three years ago, sent by my father to look for gold to help my family. All I found in the gold country was violence against Chinese. The whites only allowed Chinese to file claims for mines already worked. Some Chinese were clever enough to sift dirt under the cabins for gold which fell through the floorboards. Unfortunately, when the whites found out, they killed the Chinese. So I feared for my life but returning to San Francisco, there were no jobs in Chinatown. Ah, too much bad news. So, why are you here alone?"*

"I've just arrived from Hong Kong. I'm here to join my brother at his shop," said the boy emotionlessly.

"How old are you and is it just you and your brother here?"

"I'm 11 and my brother is 17."

"I'm 18 and since you speak Sze Yup, you must also be from Taishan."

"You are mistaken, I'm from Canton. That is where my family lives," Lew Hing said, hesitantly.

Lew Yu responded, "I'm from Sun-Ning District and came from my village to find work but only working on the railroad was available, tough, tiring and dangerous work. The white devils needed us to work but hated us. They paid us next to nothing, calling us 'Coolies'."

Finishing their meal, Lew Yu said: "I will show you a bit of Chinatown and help you carry your baggage. We should take a walk down Dupont Street, the fanciest street in Chinatown where you can find anything and everything."

Dupont Street, c. 1870

They walked down Dupont Street, past the produce and meat stores, Lew Hing gawking at the fancy shops selling dry goods, herbs, clothing and apparel just like in Hong Kong but along the way past many shabbily dressed men, some begging, crowding the streets; and there was a noticeable absence of women. Most of all, he was startled by the dirty, overcrowding and unsanitary conditions of the street and dark alleys. This was not the image of the main thoroughfare he imagined while on the ship.

Spotting the street sign in Chinese, "Commercial Street", Lew Hing and Lew Yu bade goodbye to each other and parted company. Lew Hing turned down out of the sunlit main street into a narrow street cast in gloom. Looking up for sunlight, he saw the street lined with three- and four-story buildings on both sides, many of the buildings in rundown condition with all kinds of things hanging out of windows on makeshift poles of bamboo, clothing flapping in the wind and food dangling from strings attached to the poles. Only by looking straight up could one know it was daylight and not night time.

HING KEE & CO.

Arriving at 716 Commercial, and seeing the sign "Hing Kee & Co." by the entrance, he saw the store covered the ground floor of the brick building. The business must be doing well and needed help. As was the custom in Chinese culture to "keep the fertile water in house," his brother must have asked their father to send Lew Hing to join him.

Waiting quietly by the door until all the customers were served, he moved forward to the counter. Neither recognized each other as years had passed since Lew Hing had been sent to Hong Kong by their father. In fact, Lew Hing did not even know that his older half-brother by his father's first wife was married and had a wife and son in Canton.

Lew Hing greeted his brother. *"It's been years since we last saw each other. We thank you for the money you have sent back to help the family. Here is a letter from our father."*

His brother opened the letter, read it intently then remarked to Lew Hing, *"It is good news that my wife and child are well, I miss them so. It is also good that third mother is well and second brother and fourth brother and your sisters are doing well despite the famine and drought."*

In the beginning, his brother was friendly and helping but stern and sometimes strict and demanding when instructing Lew Hing on how he wanted the books kept and the premises cleaned. His brother also used him as a stock boy, janitor, bookkeeper and errand boy to show him different aspects of running a business.

However, one of the responsibilities his brother wanted Lew Hing to assume was to go to the custom house brokerage to clear goods exported from China for businesses. So, as his brother had done before, a priority was for Lew Hing to attend missionary school to learn English. Regardless of the chores assigned, he was always given time off to attend school.

Both the opportunity to interact with the customs house and to attend English classes would be important cornerstones in his future endeavors.

MISSIONARY SCHOOL

Commenting in 1900 upon the dominant anti-Chinese mood of the late nineteenth century, Reverend Ira M. Condit, pastor of a Presbyterian Church mission in San Francisco's Chinatown since 1870 observed as follows:

> *"There seems to be a combination of reasons which breed and keep alive this animosity against our Mongolian brothers. Race antagonism has undoubtedly something to do with it, but the fact that they do not assimilate with us has more. They constitute a foreign substance cast into our social order, which will not mingle, but keeps up a constant irritation. The amount of irritation depends upon the size of the disturbing mass. A few Chinamen would have no perceptible effect. They could be easily digested by the national stomach....But multiply units*

> *by millions, and the matter becomes exceedingly serious. Hence the fear of their pouring in upon us in overwhelming crowds has had much to do with our attitude towards them."*[4]

Western religious institutions flocked to Chinatown for the opportunity to proselytize in hopes of saving the "Celestials." Part of the effort involved running mission schools to teach English. For example, the Presbyterian Church ran a school with an estimated total enrollment at 5,500. Many, if not most, were young men, sons of Chinese merchants learning English as part of their business training.

The classes at the missionary school were valuable as Lew Hing learned not only English but also the difficulties of being Chinese in America. What his father had told him years ago became more clear as he learned about the hatred of the whites toward the Chinese. It would have a profound effect on how he would approach realizing his dream.

Lew Hing pondered the information of how racial discrimination colored the perception of whites towards Chinese. He knew this was important because to be truly successful in business required a larger market and that market was the white market. The key, given the increasing anti-Chinese sentiment towards Chinese, was whites would work with the yellows if the only color concerned was green.

Lew Hing would attend class at night and bring his books to the shop and study when he had free time during the day.

Noticing his dedication in class, the teacher asked, "What will you do once you've learned English, Hing?"

---

[4] Condit, Ira M., *The Chinaman as We See Him* (Chicago: Fleming H. Revell Co., 1900), p. 21.

"I want to be a successful businessman in America," Lew Hing replied.

Lew Hing also asked the teacher for as many books explaining American business practices as were available, which he assiduously devoured.

To better understand how business was done outside of Chinatown, when business was slow at the shop, he would wander in the white business and shopping districts to familiarize himself with American culture and to look for products which might appeal to Chinese consumers.

Different from his brother, Lew Hing was forward-looking, thinking how to improve the profitability of the store. His brother had complained about the Sam Yup merchants' monopoly, which allowed them to undercut Sze Yup merchants' prices for the same products. Lew Hing thought that one way to beat the competition was to introduce some white-made products that might appeal to Chinese.

Initially hesitant to speak with the whites, he knew that the only way to improve his English and learn about business was to engage whenever possible.

As a young boy, rarely did he attract attention from whites while wandering about, particularly wearing white man's clothing and not having a queue at the time. Even shopkeepers did not turn him away when he went into shops. He always used his perfect English to disarm them into speaking with him.

"Excuse me, Reverend Condit of the Presbyterian missionary school has given his students an assignment and that assignment is to interview a successful business to see how it runs. Is it possible for me to interview you?"

Using this ruse, Lew Hing was able to fill notebooks full of questions for which he wanted answers from unsuspecting white business owners.

Constantly looking for new products, he spied canned meat, vegetables and fruits being sold in white stores and wondered whether the products could be sold to Chinese making the long voyage back to China.

Returning the next day, he approached the store clerk and asked to see the store manager. With his story of how his business teacher had assigned students to interview store buyers, he inquired if the buyer was available to answer some questions. Invariably, the white store workers were happy to openly answer his questions.

Intrigued with the idea of canned food, Lew Hing would file this away among the many business ideas swirling in his head as possibilities for future business, ready to be considered if and when a right time might appear.

BEGINNING A FRIENDSHIP

1871

Above the din of the crowded sidewalks, the competing Sam Yup and Sze Yup dialects, one sounding like birds in spring and the other, like the harsh guttural sound of a rake across a gravel path in a beautiful garden, Lew Hing heard a voice shouting in Sze Yup: *"Lew Hing! Hey, Lew Hing! How are you?"*

Looking in the direction of the voice he saw a man waving to him. Not recognizing him at first, then crossing the street towards him, he broke into a wide smile as he recognized Lew Yu and exclaimed, *"Lew Yu! It's good to see you. What have you been doing? Where have you been?"*

Lew Yu responded: *"I've been working in a cannery up north, a salmon cannery. There are many Chinese working during the canning season. It is tough traveling to the canneries in Alaska because the whites hate us so we travel in groups and the whites are afraid to attack us. But the money is good and after I send some money home, I have enough to live on for the rest of the year if I'm careful. Of course, I occasionally go to the brothels, gambling houses and opium dens."* Lew Yu said with a wink. Lew Yu then asked Lew Hing how he had been since they last had a meal at the restaurant nearly a year ago.

"I have read about the hatred of Chinese by whites. I can read English newspapers now, having attended missionary school almost since I came. It is a pity that we come looking for opportunities and want to live in peace but I read almost daily about our countrymen fleeing the towns here and up north where the white mobs have murdered men, raped women and burned Chinatowns to the ground. Every day more and more refugees come to Chinatown; it is getting so crowded and the living conditions are so bad since the white landlords refuse to keep up their buildings.

"If there is any good news, my brother's store is one of the few owned and run by our kind and most of the refugees are from our area, Taishan, so they feel more comfortable shopping at a Sze Yup store. Because many lost everything when they fled, they came here with only the clothes on their backs. So, I convinced my brother to extend credit and after he initially said no, we tried out a credit system and haven't lost any money! Because of this, we are busier than ever.

"You know, since we last parted, I haven't had time other than for work and school so I have no one to talk with but my brother. Come back with me to my brother's store. He needs some additional employees and since you also come from Sun-Ning district, he may feel comfortable talking with you."

By 1872, Hing Kee & Co. was running smoothly with Lew Hing handling the books, ordering and with sufficient

English fluency, dealing with the newly established Bellingall Custom House located near Chinatown at 425 Battery Street. Word had spread through the Chinatown merchant community that P.W. Bellingall was cordial and solicitous and treated them in a respectful manner.

Lew Yu proved to be a hard worker, attending to customers during busy times, and in off time, stocking shelves and performing general clean-up duties. The three of them would cook, eat and sleep in the quarters at the back of the store.

In August, 1872, Lew Hing's older brother decided he could leave the business without worry to visit his wife and son in Canton. He booked on the *PSS America*, the first and most expensive vessel among the Pacific Mail Steamship Company's "China Line."

FATE INTERVENES

1872

When built, the *PSS America* had a passenger capacity of 93 with a crew of 103. "Launched in 1869, it traveled around the Cape of Good Hope without passengers and used its sails for a large part of the trip. At Singapore, *PSS America* began to pick up Chinese for steerage passage and eventually arrived in San Francisco on October 20, 1869 with 730 immigrants."[5]

On this voyage Lew Hing's brother joined 657 other Chinese in steerage for the journey to Asia when tragedy struck.

---

[5] Von Earl of Cruise. *History - Pacific Mail Steamship Company*, earlofcruise.blogspot.com, July 20, 2017

"The Pacific Mail paddle steamship *AMERICA PSS* was lying at anchor in the harbour of Yokohama on the night of August 24, 1872, when she caught fire. She had on board many hundreds of passengers, chiefly Chinese returning from California, and a

Postcard Drawing of a Pacific Mail Steamship, c. 1870s

valuable cargo, part of which was 1,600,000 Mexican dollars. The fire spread with terrible swiftness and within a few hours the vessel was burned to the water's edge.

Boats from ships in the harbour rendered prompt assistance but between 60 and 70 persons lost their lives. Many of the unfortunate Chinese were drowned owing to their persistence in clinging to the wooden boxes containing the money they had saved while in California."[6]

When the fire broke out, the ship had unloaded all the passengers except the Chinese bound for Hong Kong and Singapore. While trying to escape the fire, they crowded the ladder, collapsing it and throwing many of the passengers into the cold water in the darkness of night.

When Lew Hing's older brother failed to show up in Canton, his father knew something was amiss. And when the passenger list along with the news of the tragedy was made known and his name was not on the manifest from Japan to Hong Kong, wailing within the walls of the Lew household began in earnest.

Elder brother's widow and son were inconsolable. Her mother-in-law, first wife and now the son, her husband were dead. What would be her fate and that of her son?

Her father-in-law and third wife prepared for a funeral without the body. They consulted with Buddhist monks to prepare to appropriately venerate his existence to ensure in the afterlife that his spirit is placated.

There was a mourning period during which elder brother Lew's widow and son wore white mourning clothing prescribed by the Buddhist monk. A ceremony was performed to transfer food, money and other symbolic goods from the living to the dead, and another ceremony was held to install a spirit tablet for him along with the playing of music to settle the spirit.

Finally, the family held a funeral procession with his son carrying a picture of his father leading the procession, trailed behind by his mother wailing her grief. Later, a feast

---

[6] Hocking Charles, *Dictionary of Disasters at Sea during the Age of Steam*. Lloyd's Register of Shipping. 1969.

for the family members marked the formal conclusion of the mourning process.

Lew Hing promised to take care of his elder brother's wife and son for life.

THREE

THE YEARS OF GROWTH 1872 - 1903

ACCEPTING NEW RESPONSIBILITIES 1872

Once his older brother had left for China in 1872, Lew Hing, at the age of 14 grew up fast, now faced with the responsibility of running the family store and carrying out the responsibility previously taken care of by his brother, remitting money to support the Lew family in Canton. With his brother deceased, the pressure was even more intense. Fortunately, Lew Yu-tang was there to help.

As the Sam Yup merchants continued their control on pricing of exported goods through their monopoly in China, which allowed for lower prices to the consumers but higher profits, Lew Hing looked for ways to make money. In school, he learned about stock companies and investment opportunities not only in property (difficult for Chinese to buy) but in white companies through buying shares that were reasonably priced.

Since only Lew Hing spoke, read and wrote English, he transacted business for Hing Kee with the customs house and in the process became friends with P.W. Bellingall. After one particular meeting over business in 1874, Lew Hing asked, *"Mr. Bellingall, sir, may I ask a question about investing as you appear very sophisticated in such an area?"*

Intrigued, Bellingall responded, "How can I help you, Hing?"

"Can you please tell me about investment in stocks and teach me about investment strategies?"

Flattered, Bellingall began tutoring Lew Hing. *"We are lucky as the Comstock Lode is experiencing a second boom with the Consolidated Virginia Mine opening up. It is a good time to invest in mining stocks."*

From the beginning, they formed an enduring relationship, which grew from business to become personal. In this context, Lew Hing sought advice from Bellingall about investing in stocks and when he was of minimum age, he purchased an onlooker's seat in the board of mining stockbrokers.

Lew Hing's foray into the world of investing in stocks was not without its ups and downs. He and Bellingall, along with thousands of others, purchased stocks in companies mining silver. They were unfazed in 1875 when there was a run on the Bank of California that closed the three stock exchanges and thousands lost money. But when, in 1877, two of the Comstock mines closed and his stocks became worthless, Lew Hing had learned a bitter lesson; no investment is safe unless he had direct control of its fate.

P.W. Bellingall, in his unpublished memoirs housed at the University of California Bancroft Library, would describe Lew Hing as "one of my very best friends" and went on to say "No white man on earth could have been a kinder friend than Lew Hing has been to me."[7] Considering Bellingall as close to a white fatherly figure in his life, Lew Hing would reward him later in life with a seat on the board of directors of Pacific Coast Cannery and profits from two offshoot canneries controlled by Pacific Coast Cannery, San Pablo Cannery Co. and Crescent Cannery Co.

Counseling Lew Hing to always keep an eye on direct competition, Bellingall suggested in 1873 that Lew Hing look to expand the products sold in his store. Lew Hing would wander into a competitor's stores to find what was selling. At Hep Yuen, at 915 Dupont Street, a Sam Yup merchant-run dry goods store, he saw tin ware for sale and saw it was a big seller. Finding a supplier, Hing Kee became the only store catering to Sze Yup to carry tin ware.[8]

One day, Lew Hing was chatting with Bellingall, "Mr. Bellingall...." Bellingall interrupted, "Call me Peter from now on, please, we are too good of friends to be so formal."

"You are right...Peter. Well, I'm interested in branching out beyond the store and I have an idea in what direction I want to go. I also want to reward my friend, Lew Yu for his hard work and dedication to making the store such a success. I would like to make him a partner in Hing Kee."

"Hing, that's a good idea. You will have a partner who has a stake in the store so he will do his best to keep it successful while you look for other opportunities. And since you have been doing the ordering, bookkeeping and receipts daily, you need not worry about the finances of the store."

---

[7] Bellingall, P.W., Unpublished memoirs. Bancroft Library, University of California, Berkeley

[8] Well's Fargo & Co. *Directory of Chinese Merchants, San Francisco and Sacramento 1873*, Britton & Rey, San Francisco.

Returning to the store, Lew Hing and Lew Yu sat down as they did daily after closing:

"Lew Yu, you have been such a dedicated and hard worker in helping make the store a success. I would like to offer you a partnership in the store based on your efforts before and in the future in lieu of paying any money."

Lew Yu was astonished and grateful for the offer and enthusiastically accepted. With this gesture, Lew Hing's thought wasn't entirely altruistic; he would have a loyal and uncompromising friend for life if he were ever in need.

When Lew Hing took on Lew Yu as a partner, Bellingall recommended he take out an announcement in the San Francisco Examiner announcing this. Bellingall said a business announcing a partnership in a white newspaper was a sign that the business was so successful that it was ready for major expansion. In this way, Lew Hing was telling his competition that Hing Kee & Co. was a business on the rise.

CERTIFICATE OF PARTNERSHIP. — I certify that I constitute a partnership transacting business in this State; its principal place of business is San Francisco, California; its name is HING KEE & CO. Name and place of residence signed hereto. May 30, 1874.
LEW HING, of San Francisco, California.
[Seal.] SAMUEL S. MURFEY, Notary Public.
WM. HARNEY, County Clerk.
je1 4wM By W. Stevenson, Deputy Clerk.

Announcement in the *San Francisco Examiner*
June 1, 8 and 15, 1874

Having secured the stability of Hing Kee, Lew Hing began reviewing the possibilities for another business, one that would be an entrée into the white business world. He was stumped until during their nightly meeting, Lew Yu said,

"Hing, you know tin containers for food is a new and growing industry. Canned food can be kept longer without spoiling, can be transported safely and is useful in all situations. Think about the possibility of supplying food to people in a disaster or troops at war."

Lew Hing saw the possibilities and would share the idea with Bellingall. After listening at their next meeting, Bellingall agreed that there would be a demand for canned food in the future and said, *"I think it's a good idea but will require considerable learning. If you want to build a business producing canned food, you need to be an expert at two things, tin can making and food processing."*

Lew Hing decided he needed to learn to be a tinsmith and said to Lew Yu, *"If you run the store, I will find a metal shop to learn tin making and carry out my responsibilities of ordering, bookkeeping and duties at night. If necessary, we can hire additional help to stock the shelves and clean the store."*

Lew Yu responded enthusiastically as he knew that while there were more customers, it was becoming more difficult to get rich as the Sam Yup merchants continued to cause headaches for Sze Yup merchants with their monopoly on the supply side.

It was 1875 and Bellingall found a tin shop willing to take Lew Hing on as a shop boy. It didn't pay much but that was not his purpose, which was to learn the trade. He could live frugally and had money coming from Hing Kee.

Lew Hing enjoyed the walk to the tin shop, which was located in another part of San Francisco. It gave him an opportunity to walk in forbidden areas of San Francisco and, with an employee card in his pocket, if he were stopped, he could simply tell the police that he was going to work and show them the card to see. In addition, despite the anti-Chinese atmosphere and the roaming white hoodlums, he was left alone mainly because at nearly seventeen years old, he was unusually tall and large for his age, taller and larger than many white men.

Lew Hing worked diligently at his job, was willing and eager to help when needed. His English was more polished, not the stilted English of school but the English spoken by native whites. The white owner was impressed with Lew Hing as a hard worker and his ability to speak English almost as well as a white man. He quickly found an eager trainee.

After two years, Lew Hing felt he had learned all that could be learned in the white shop. In 1877 he set up a metal shop on the third floor of a three-story brick building across the street from Hing Kee & Co. at 715 Commercial Street. Once he had set up the operation and perfected the tin cans for salmon, Bellingall arranged for a contract from a cannery in the Pacific Northwest.

Lew Hing and P.W. Bellingall went into business together making tin cans for the cannery. Bellingall, as the front man, dealt with the white tin suppliers, warehousemen, money men and sales agents. When the business ran into a severe cash flow problem, Bellingall co-signed loan papers with no collateral other than his word.

Bellingall was also helpful in other ways. By virtue of his business and familiarity with some customs inspectors, when customs seized goods from China for whatever reason, Bellingall was notified and he would alert Lew Hing. Instead of being destroyed by customs, many times goods could be bought at a deep discount. These goods were never sold through Hing Kee but sold to other Sze Yup shops.

Having this friendship with Bellingall was an epiphany for Lew Hing, confirming his belief that to get ahead, he needed to work extensively with whites.

1876 SMALLPOX EPIDEMIC

An event of significant proportions would cause Lew Hing to pause and consider its impact on his business: the smallpox epidemic in the white community in 1876. The white city officials blamed the Chinese.

In 1870, the San Francisco Board of Health was reorganized as a distinct political unit with considerable power within the city. Not only did it supervise the administration of the city hospitals, the jail, the correctional school (the industrial school) and the quarantine system for the harbor, it also appointed a city health official to oversee health and sanitary conditions within San Francisco.[9]

While public health medical professionals were chosen from among the best trained members of the medical community, the range of municipal problems with which they were confronted was often beyond the scope of their medical expertise. In the absence of hard scientific evidence, the pronouncements of the board and the health officer were often characterized by political or social expedience.

Unable to pinpoint the specific mode of transmission of a disease, the public health officials relied on the miasmatic theory of disease popular in the 1870s; epidemic outbreaks were caused either by the state of the atmosphere or by poor sanitary conditions affecting the local atmosphere.

---

[9] J. Marion Read and Mary E. Mathes, *History of the San Francisco Medical Society: 1850 -1900*. 1958 (San Francisco: San Francisco Medical Society), 1:57.

Cartoon from *The Wasp*, May 26, 1882, depicting myth of rampant disease in Chinatown

"The obvious culprit was Chinatown, with its foul and disgusting vapors, as the primary source of atmospheric pollution within the city. Numerous citations were issued by the health authorities for such sanitary offenses as generating unwholesome odors, improper disposal of garbage, faulty construction of privy vaults and drains, and failure to clean market stalls."[10]

---

[10] Workingmen's Party of California, Anti-Chinese Council, *Chinatown Declared a Nuisance* (San Francisco, 1880), p.5 of 16 pages; 3x5 inch pamphlet

To these sanitarians of the 1870s, Chinatown was more than a slum. It was "a laboratory of infection," populated by "lying and treacherous" aliens who had minimal regard for the health of the American people.

In 1875 and 1876, when a virulent smallpox epidemic struck San Francisco, the white officials laid the blame on the doorstep of Chinatown. The city health officer ordered every house in Chinatown to be thoroughly fumigated. Nevertheless, the epidemic raged on, resulting in some 1,646 reported cases with 405 deaths among the white population of San Francisco.[11]

Unable to account for the severity of the epidemic, the city health officer, J.L. Meares, offered the following explanation: "I unhesitatingly declare my belief that the cause is the presence in our midst of 30,000 (as a class) of unscrupulous, lying and treacherous Chinamen, who have disregarded our sanitary laws, concealed and are concealing their cases of smallpox."[12]

There were medical professionals who mocked the political and social pronouncements of the city health board and city health officers: "The Chinese were the focus of Caucasian animosities, and they were made responsible for mishaps in general. A destructive earthquake would probably be charged to their account."[13]

Despite the general acceptance of the germ theory in the 1880s challenging the belief that epidemic outbreaks were directly attributable to conditions within Chinatown, it did little to bring to the end the miasmatic theory.

---

[11] *Municipal Reports*, 1877, p.394.

[12] *Ibid.*, 1877, p.397.

[13] *Pacific Medical and Surgical Journal*, 19 (June, 1876) pp. 36-37.

"The "germ" theory of disease is now an acknowledged fact in the science of medicine....This theory teaches us that material like cloth, tobacco, food, if exposed to the atmosphere charged with those germs, is infected by them, and thus detrimental to the health of the wearer or consumer of such merchandise. The dangerous result of such evil, we hold, is practically proven by the ravages of diseases like diphtheria, etc., in this city, irrespective of time, season or places. The physician who tries to trace the source of the infection is mostly always unable to do so, and *we believe that the existing evils in Chinatown are the proper source."* (emphasis added by author)[14]

A LEARNING EXPERIENCE

In 1876, Lew Hing was walking home late one night down a dimly lit street, listening to the sound of music and clack of tiles from a gambling den. Carrying the day's receipts from the sale of goods from customs to some shops in Chinatown, suddenly two men sprang from the shadows of a doorway and surrounded him; they carried hand axes.

One, clearly the leader, spoke, *"Give me all your money and be quick."*

Lew Hing handed over the bag and watched them run away. The next day, he purchased a five-shot revolver and, without altering his routine, waited for the robbers to show up again.

Several days later, the robbers once again cornered him, this time from a different doorway. But there was a third man with the two who had robbed him before. Despite covering

[14] Workingmen's Party of California, Anti-Chinese Council, *Chinatown Declared a Nuisance!* (San Francisco, 1880) p.13

their faces, Lew Hing recognized two from the clothing they had worn before.

"This is easy," the leader cackled before Lew Hing stepped back and pulled out his gun.

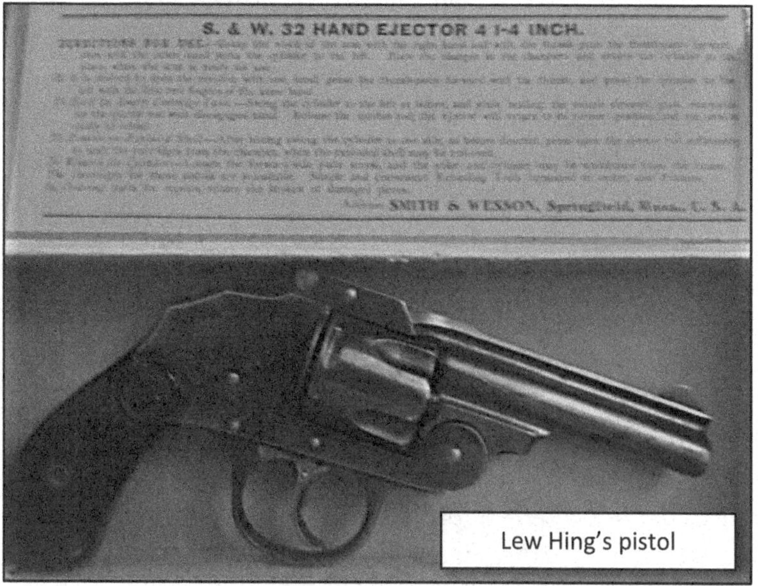

Lew Hing's pistol

"Drop the axes and line up against the wall. Keep your hands up. Motioning to the leader, he said, "You step forward."

As the leader stepped forward, Lew Hing pointed at his head and without hesitation pulled the trigger. The roar of the gun caused the other two to look in horror and then away as the body hit the ground with a thud, blood spurting from the third eye. Lew Hing then stepped towards the second robber who had robbed him before and shot him in the head as well.

He then turned towards the third one, the taller and more husky of the two:

"I want you to tell anyone who thinks about robbing me that this is what they will get." Lew Hing said. He watched

the shaken man rapidly walk off, feeling nauseated as he took a deep breath.

Shaking as he returned to his room, Lew Hing reached for a glass and gulped down rice wine. Looking at the gun he wondered how he had the guts to do what he had done. After calming down, he reconciled the fact that he had within him no qualms about how to address a problem so long as it came with a message.

Days later, the third robber appeared at his store, eyes cast to the floor and humbled as he spoke:

"I beg your forgiveness for my part in robbing you. I didn't know it was you. If there is any way I might repay you for my dishonorable behavior, I pledge on my life to do so."

Lew Hing looked in astonishment: "Ah Chew! What fate have the gods given you?"

Ah Chew replied, "I couldn't find work on my own so I signed up with a labor contractor. I was working digging caves out of solid rock for wineries. We were to be paid when the work was finished but the labor contractor and the owner of the mines tricked us. When we went to the white owner to demand payment, he and other whites chased us off with guns and because the law forbade us from testifying in court, all hope was lost."

Lew Hing interrupted him and said, "You are an honorable man, driven to desperation by the times; you saved my life once and now it is my turn to return the favor. I will give you a job working in my business."

Ah Chew would work with Lew Hing in the tin shop and accompany him while he made the rounds serving as his bodyguard. Ah Chew learned to be a tinsmith after which Lew Hing would send him home to China with both a trade and considerable savings to support his family.

U.S. CONGRESS PASSES PAGE ACT LIMITING ENTRY OF CHINESE WOMEN

1875

On February 18, 1875, Congressman Horace F. Page of California introduced H.R. 4747 to prohibit entry of cheap Chinese labor and immoral Chinese women into the United States. Signed into law on March 3, 1875, the Page Act of 1875 was the first restrictive federal immigration law in the United States. It effectively limited the entry of Chinese women, marking the end of open borders.

The process of entry for any Chinese woman was to successfully negotiate a byzantine scheme devised by the American consul in Hong Kong, David Bailey, who had pushed hard for the Act. The scheme assumed all applicants were would-be prostitutes, and subjected an applicant to four interviews before the American consul would issue a certificate required by the Page Act declaring the applicant was not emigrating for "lewd or immoral purposes." Only then can a shipping ticket be purchased. On the day of sailing, the harbor-master interrogated the applicant again before stamping her arm with printer's ink for identification on board. Even then, an on-board interrogation by the American consul was held. Once the ship arrived in San Francisco, officials would interrogate the applicant and if satisfied, issue a certificate stating the applicant was not "immigrating for the purposes of prostitution."[15] Only then was the applicant allowed to land.

---

[15] Abrams, Kerry, *Polygamy, Prostitution, and the Federalization of Immigration Law,* Columbia Law Review, April 2005, 105 (3): 641-716)

LEW HING MARRIED IN ABSENTIA

1877

The Page Act was a serious impediment to a Chinese wife joining her husband in the United States. Lew Hing and his promised bride faced this problem when, in 1877, he and Chin Hao were to be married in accordance with promises both sets of parents had made years before when Lew Hing was twelve and Chin Hao ten.

Chin Hao was the daughter of a herbalist in Canton. The family lived on the same street as Lew Hing's family. Born October 13, 1860 she was two and a half years younger than Lew Hing, who was born May 26, 1858. She grew up on the same block in Canton but was unlikely to know of him as he was sent to Hong Kong as a young child for his formal education. Like Lew Hing, she was Sze Yup but from a different district: Xin Hui. She had bound feet, reflecting a privileged upbringing. Like many girls from well-to-do families, she was not taught to read or write, as the assumption was that all the mundane matters requiring literacy could be handled by servants or her future husband. As such, she had no formal education as girls were not given the opportunity to go to school.

The fact that Lew Hing was busy with work and would not be present at the wedding in China was culturally acceptable. Chinese custom had provided an alternative, given that so many men were "Sojourners", forced to look for work overseas to earn money and frequently difficult for them to return to marry in person. Traditional rituals associated with marriage were performed in China with Lew Hing represented by a rooster. Chinese wedding guests gave "red envelopes" filled with money for the newlywed couple; a dowry of money and gifts was provided by Chin Hao's family. A tea ceremony was performed before a brief wedding ceremony in Canton after which a lavish wedding banquet took place.

Why a rooster? In ancient China, when a groom couldn't be present at his wedding, a rooster was chosen to represent him, and it was placed alongside the bride during the ceremony. The choice of the rooster was auspicious for Lew Hing and Chin Hao (now Chin *Shee*, her married name) because in Chinese culture, roosters suggest prosperity and as they reproduce very fast, Chinese believe this to represent prosperity in terms of both population and wealth. They would have eight children.

CHIN SHEE SUCCESSFULLY ARRIVES IN THE UNITED STATES

1877

The procedure devised by American consul Bailey in enforcing the provisions of the Page Act achieved its purpose; while 385 Chinese women qualified for entry in 1875, after the passage of the Act, only 77 qualified for entry in 1877. One who gained entry was Chin Shee. Traveling to Hong Kong with Lew Hing's mother, she appeared alone at the American consulate. The process was not for the faint hearted but Chin Shee (married name), barely sixteen with no knowledge of English, managed to successfully pass each grueling step.

Lew Hing's mother, granted permission to accompany Chin Shee, then escorted her to San Francisco on a Pacific steamship paddle wheeler. During the voyage, his mother forbade Chin Shee to leave her cabin, lest she might meet a new suitor aboard the ship. Of course, the rooster went along as well.

When the ship landed, Lew Hing was waiting at the dockside with Ah Chew by the gangplank. As his mother and future bride walked down off the ship, he rushed forward to greet them while Ah Chew took their baggage.

"My son, you have grown so tall and big since I last saw you in Hong Kong. Look at your lovely bride, Chin Shee, how beautiful she is."

Chin Shee, shy and tentative, bowed to Lew Hing, admiring his fine clothing as it indicated she would have a comfortable life.

Lew Hing and his mother walked first, with Chin Shee next to Ah Chew following behind, silently surveying her new community. Lew Hing showed his mother and his bride to their new apartment at 715 Commercial Street where they would stay until his mother would return to China. Lew Hing stayed across the street at 716 Commercial, in the back of the store.

Lew Hing's mother took charge of the arrangements for the second marriage ceremony. She met with the owner of the finest Chinese restaurant in Chinatown to make the reservation. She had brought the Chinese wedding invitations to be used to invite the friends. Because she could neither read or write, Lew Hing filled in the details of the red wedding envelope, with gold, vertical wording read from right to left with the groom's information presented first before the bride's and the double happiness symbol. The invitation included the Chinese calendar dates for the wedding banquet, order of birth and names of the bride and groom, names of the parents, dinner venue, time for the cocktail reception and time for dinner.

On the day of the wedding, Chin Shee wore a red dress, a "qipao" and covered her face with a red veil, red symbolizing happiness, prosperity and good luck.

The wedding banquet was quite lavish. The guests, including P.W. Bellingall, signed their names on a scroll to present their gifts. There were six courses: *Lobster and Chicken* represented yin and yang, the groom and bride; *Scallops*, as the name of the scallop in Chinese is a homophone for the phrase "raising or bringing a child into your life"; and *Abalone and Sea Cucumber*, abalone being associated with the word "abundance" while sea cucumber means "good heart" in Cantonese. Lew Hing's mother also included three more dishes in the banquet because they symbolize abundance and love needed to avoid conflicts: A whole *Duck*, symbolizing fidelity and representing peace, unity and completeness in the marriage; *Noodles,* symbolizing a long and happy marriage; and finally a whole *Fish,* which in Chinese sounds identical to the word for "abundance".

His mother stayed a month, giving the new bride advice and suggestions. Satisfied that her son and his new bride were settled, she returned to China.

ANTI-CHINESE RIOT IN SAN FRANCISCO 1877

Chin Shee's arrival in a new land during the Smallpox Plague was likely unsettling but the next year, a more dangerous plague of a different kind emerged: the plague of disgruntled white workers. They would take out their frustrations against Chinese in the form of rioting. In the midst of the depression, workers in the East struck against the wealthy ruling class, leading workers in the West to begin agitating. Following the rail strike in Pittsburgh, then Baltimore and spreading to other cities, leaders of San Francisco unions called for a unity meeting to support the strikers in all the eastern cities on July 23, 1877.

Meeting at the corner of Grove and Larkin, many in the crowd had another agenda besides supporting the strikers in the East. Even though James F. D'Arcy, who helped create a national Workingmen's Party and was elected to run the meeting, stated that this was not an "anti-Coolie" meeting, the crowd shouted, *"Talk about the Chinamen!"* and *"Give us the Coolie business!"*

Cartoon from *The Wasp*, December 5, 1877:
"The First Blow at the Chinese Question"

Soon, the disaffected men, several hundred in number, broke away from the rally, led by "the hoodlum element", a term coined in San Francisco in 1866. By 1877 the term described gangs that frequently attacked Chinese residents. On this night in July, they charged through the center of the city, attacking more than a dozen Chinese homes and businesses, mostly laundries. The violence continued for three nights and spread south of Market and out to the Western Addition. In anticipation of being targeted, businesses took down their signs and put up blinds, making them look like ordinary residences. Rioters still targeted more Chinese homes and businesses and threatened establishments that employed Chinese workers.

Alarmed over the unrest which threatened to spread to the East Bay, California Governor Irwin called for military help and the Army issued 2,000 rifles to the newly formed Committee of Safety to help contain the violence. The climax of the riots was a battle on the slopes of Rincon Hill between the rock-throwing hoodlums and members of the Committee, many armed with pick handles. Several people died and dozens were injured.

This violent confrontation was the spark that ignited a movement to once and for all settle "the Chinese question" on one hand, and to redress workers' grievances with the wealthy on the other. The movement, now called the Workingmen's Party of California, gained momentum thanks to a silver-tongued street orator, Denis Kearney. In addition to his call to throw the rich and powerful out of office, break up monopoly land holdings, redistribute wealth through heavy taxes and "provide for the poor and unfortunate, the weak, the helpless, and especially the young," he advocated throwing out the Chinese. Kearney's style was to call for immediate drastic action to attain the party's goals, hence his rallying cry, "The Chinese Must Go!'

CHINA ESTABLISHES A CONSULATE IN SAN FRANCISCO

1878

Chinese Consulate, 806 Stockton St., San Francisco

Responding to the repeated requests of the Chinese for an official agency to protect them from the growing hostility in California, in 1878, the Chinese government established a consulate in San Francisco. Its charge was to protect its citizens from the anti-Chinese attacks and provide leadership for the Chinese-American community. The consul proved an ardent advocate of Chinese rights, protesting against discriminatory laws and demanding investigations and reparations when Chinese became victims of white mobs. While not always sharing the perspectives of the Chinese immigrants, the consul did exercise significant political power in the community, such as attempting to mediate internal conflicts within San Francisco's Chinatown between the Sam Yup and Sze Yup.

In challenging discriminatory laws, the Chinese consul was instrumental in developing the litigation strategy, providing funding for the legal battles and hiring an American lawyer, Frederick A. Bee, to serve as vice consul. The consulate also kept other attorneys on retainer, including Thomas Riordan, to represent Chinese when the need arose.

As Lew Hing would begin to develop his business interests in the future, cultivation of relationships with the consul general and white lawyers would help him realize his dream of competing with white competition. The fact that his later business, Pacific Fruit Packing Company, eventually surrounded the Chinese consulate on Stockton Street from 1888 to 1902 aided in cultivating these relationships.

CALIFORNIA LEADERS ATTEMPT TO LIMIT IMPACT OF CHINESE ON ITS ECONOMY

1870s - 1880s

While Lew Hing dreamed of a new business to complement Hing Kee, he was keenly aware that starting any new business which targeted a market outside Chinatown would bring scrutiny from white competitors. While confident he could outmaneuver competition, he knew that his efforts might be adversely affected by one source over which he had no control, the white political structure.

California during the 1870s and 1880s was buffeted by a series of economic downturns and competition from the East that left California businesses searching for new routes to prosperity. They had pinned their hopes on the Transcontinental Railroad, which when finished would finally link the state with larger national and international markets. Instead, the railroad imported the eastern boom-and-bust business cycle just in time to transmit the effects of the Panic of 1873 and its financial collapse west. Along with the economic misery, the railroad also brought a tidal wave of immigration: between 1870 and 1880, California's population increased by more than 50 percent. At the same time, the now-completed railroad was discharging thousands of workers. Worse still, the railroad also carried cheap Eastern goods west, forcing many of California's once-isolated industries to close their doors, making work difficult to find.

As the state absorbed these blows, the Comstock Lode experienced its second boom in as many decades. The Comstock, seated along the California-Nevada border, was the richest deposit of silver in the world and should have pumped much needed cash into the California economy. Instead, rampant speculation in mining stocks drained capital away from local industries, worsening the depression.

When the Consolidated Virginia Mine opened in 1874, speculation boosted its aggregate value by $1 million a day for two straight months. The ensuing craze induced wild fluctuations on San Francisco's three stock exchanges, varying the aggregate value by as much as $139 million in a single month in a market never valued at more than $240 million. In such an atmosphere, panics were inevitable.

In 1875, a run on the Bank of California, the state's most trusted financial institution, temporarily closed the stock exchanges and impoverished thousands. The final crash came in 1877 when the stock of the two largest Comstock mines suffered a combined loss of $140 million, or $1,000 for every adult male in San Francisco. The shock of these crashes rippled through the California economy, causing twelve bank failures in the second half of the decade and 451 business failures in 1877 alone.

Even as California's economy stalled, the rate of Chinese immigration to the state increased. Under the influence and protections of the Burlingame Treaty, the Chinese population of California jumped by 50 percent in the 1870s, rising from 49,310 to 75,218, or nearly nine percent of the total population. Because the vast majority of these new immigrants were young men of working age, their impact on labor markets was magnified well beyond their actual numbers. While Chinese immigrants may never have amounted to more than 10 percent of the total population in nineteenth century California, they could amount to as much as a third of the adult male work force. To white workers desperately seeking employment in a collapsing economy, rising numbers of Chinese laborers willing to work for lower wages seemed a real threat. For frustrated white workers, Chinese immigrants also made obvious targets as scapegoats.

The combination of economic distress and rising immigration led labor organizations and even some business owners to pressure government officials at all levels for some kind of relief. At the state level, their agitation meant success for a long-simmering movement which lobbied the legislature to deal with California's mounting social and economic complexity. The legislature responded by rewriting the state's constitution. At the constitutional convention in 1878, members of the virulently anti-Chinese Workingmen's Party of California successfully lobbied for the inclusion of some of the harshest measures ever enacted against Chinese immigrants, including one passage prohibiting corporations chartered in California from employing Chinese. White workers who hoped that these measures would finally end their misery by removing Chinese laborers from the state's economy saw their hopes dashed when federal courts quickly struck down the new measures.

The failure to contain Chinese economic and social influence at the state level convinced many white Californians that only federal legislation could once and for all rid the state of the Chinese "menace." Both the Democratic and Republican state parties exhorted their national representatives to redouble their efforts against Chinese immigration by passing a Chinese exclusion act. At the same time, white Californians also recognized that federal legislation was often slow in coming, particularly when it came to issues in western states, and even more so when it was largely supported by the working classes.

A general lack of faith in the federal government led white Californians to supplement their national efforts with more intense and vigorous harassment of the Chinese locally.

> "In San Francisco, where fully one-quarter of the state's Chinese were crowded into the city's Chinatown, officials initiated a campaign of civic harassment that would last for two decades. Throughout the 1870s and into the 1880s, the city passed ordinances designed to make life difficult for Chinese in San Francisco. Chinese labor activities such as fishing and vegetable peddling, leisure activities such as gambling and opium smoking, and even Chinese burial practices were promulgated. Regulations such as the Cubic Air Ordinance, which required 500 cubic feet of space for each occupant of a residential building, and the notorious Queue Ordinance, which required shaving the heads of inmates in the City jail, added humiliation to the harassment. Across the state, city governments wielded their vaguely defined police powers to

> strictly limit the ability, and even the right, of Chinese immigrants to earn a living in any capacity, with the intention of driving them from the state."[16]

These new laws by local and state governments differed from those targeting Chinese workers. Now, Chinese businesses were targeted. For example, legislation attempting to put Chinese laundries out of business drew a great deal of its energy from white working-class misery and agitation. Lew Hing needed to take into account ways to minimize disruption of and targeting by the whites for any business he was interested in starting.

THE UNITED STATES CONGRESS PASSES THE 1882 CHINESE EXCLUSION ACT

The western states were finally able to convince the rest of the United States that the Chinese posed a threat to the whites. Politicians from those states convinced representatives and senators of other states of the need to supplement The Page Act with laws excluding Chinese men.

American-born workers vehemently objected to the presence of and further immigration by Chinese whom they perceived as competitors for their jobs. In the 1876 national elections, both Democrat and Republican candidates took anti-Chinese immigration stances in their platforms. However, in 1879, when both houses of the U.S. Congress passed a bill to regulate Chinese immigration, President Rutherford B. Hayes vetoed it because it would violate the Burlingame Treaty.

---

[16] D. Michael Bottoms, *An Aristocracy of Color: Race and Reconstruction in California and the West, 1850-1890*. 1966 (University of Oklahoma Press: Norman), pp. 137-139.

The Burlingame Treaty was eventually annulled by subsequent American legislation and in the Spring of 1882, President Chester A. Arthur signed the Chinese Exclusion Act. The act provided an absolute 10-year moratorium on Chinese labor immigration. For the first time, Federal law proscribed entry of an ethnic working group on the premises that it endangered the good order of certain localities.

Cover of *Puck* magazine, May 17, 1882: President Chester A. Arthur pandering to the "Western Vote" for Exclusion Act

The Chinese Exclusion Act required the few non-laborers who sought entry to obtain certification from the Chinese government that they were qualified to immigrate. But this group found it increasingly difficult to prove that they were not laborers because the 1882 act defined excludables as "skilled and unskilled laborers and Chinese employed in mining." Thus very few Chinese could enter the country under the 1882 law.

The 1882 Exclusion Act also placed new requirements on Chinese who had already entered the country. If they left the United States, they had to obtain certifications to reenter. Congress, moreover, refused State and Federal courts the right to grant citizenship to Chinese resident aliens, although these courts could still deport them.

EXCLUSION ACT AFFECTS LEW HING

1883

In 1879, Lew Hing and Chin Shee welcomed their first child, a girl named Lew Yuet Yung. Her mother immediately began to bind Yuet-yung's feet.

By 1881, Chin Shee was complaining, *"I am small and Yuet-yung is getting so heavy that I am becoming so tired walking up and down three flights of stairs. In addition, she is walking now and it is dangerous to have all the tin making tools and pieces of tin where she might hurt herself."*

Lew Hing hearing her distress, moved the tin operation to 621 Jackson Street and his family to the back of Hing Kee at 716 Commercial. There the baby could walk around and the store employee could help watch her. Yuet-yung's play area was in a business environment that shaped her personality as an adult—viewing every relationship through the lens of a business person. Lew Hing continued to rent 715 Commercial to provide living quarters for Lew Yu and other employees of Hing Kee who were previously living in the back of the store.

In the early 1880s, the white mobs escalated their attacks in towns and cities, murdering men, raping women and then looting and burning the Chinatowns in towns and cities from California to Oregon, Washington, Arizona, Nevada, Idaho and Wyoming. The majority of those fleeing, Sze Yup, sought refuge in San Francisco Chinatown. They shopped at Hing Kee, giving business quite a boost.

Massacre of Chinese at Rock Springs, WY, September 2, 1885, from *Harper's Weekly*, 1886.

Needing more space to store goods to meet the increasing demand, Lew Hing moved his family out of 716 to the only available nearby space, the top floor of a four-story brick building at 707-½ Commercial Street. One can imagine the complaints by Chin Shee over this move! After several miscarriages, Chin Shee fell into a deep depression. She pressed Lew Hing to allow her to travel back to China where her mother and mother-in-law could provide some comfort. She rarely ventured out either within Chinatown or outside to Portsmouth Square. When Chin Shee did venture out with Yuet-yung, she was always accompanied by one of the employees of Hing Kee for safety. She might be mistaken by whites as a prostitute and similarly by the overwhelming number of Chinese males in Chinatown. Unable to speak English, she was instructed to show her marriage license to police patrols if stopped.

The perception of Chinese women as prostitutes was formed as early as 1854, based on a visit by a municipal committee to Chinatown and their report to the Board of Aldermen. The observation soon became a conviction and it colored the public perception of, attitude toward, and action against all Chinese women for almost a century. Lew Hing was fortunate Chin Shee immigrated before the 1882 Chinese Exclusion Act, as the act effectively limited the immigration of Chinese females to America. Even then, according to the U.S. census of 1870, females were only 7.2 percent of the total Chinese population.

Even more telling was the lack of other women with whom Chin Shee could share her concerns, worries, hopes and dreams. Statistics compiled in 1885 by members of San Francisco's Committee on the Condition of the Chinese reported that in the core area of Chinatown, bounded by California Kearney, Stockton and Broadway, Chin Shee and her daughter Yuet-yung were only two of just 57 women and 59 children living in recognizable families. In 1885, Chin Shee's spirits brightened as their first son Lew Gow was born. Still, she longed for China.

Lew Hing had sensed these feelings; however, there was a legal question of whether, as the wife of a "domiciled" Chinese merchant, she had the right of reentry into America. Once she went back to China, he feared that immigration laws might not allow her and their children to return to him.

Lew Hing sought the advice of lawyers, in particular Thomas D. Riordan and L.I. Mowry who had handled many Chinese cases. In the meeting, he detailed how he was married in absentia to Chin Shee in China while he was here in America and according to Chinese customs, the marriage was valid if a rooster was acting in his stead. She wanted to return to China with their daughter and son but there was no American proof of marriage nor a valid reentry document, how could she reenter?

The lawyer's opinion was not encouraging. The Exclusion Act required a specific document from the bearer which is issued only to the qualifying merchant, not to his wife. They could only recommend that he and Chin Shee apply for an American marriage license and wait for a favorable court decision allowing spouses of merchants to reenter.

"Mr. Lew, unfortunately, the exclusion act is specific as to what is required for a person who leaves the United States and then wishes to re-enter. They must have a 'Section 6 certificate in their name' to land. Legally, you can re-enter as you can prove you are a merchant and the government will issue you a 'Section 6 certificate,' but they can refuse entry to your wife and child as they do not have such a certificate nor could they qualify for one.

"Our opinion is that since merchants were named as one of the 'exempted classes' in each of the various exclusion laws, it follows that their wives and children were also 'exempted.' However, no such language exists in any of the exclusion acts so legally, a collector could very well deny entry to your wife and child if they went back to China for a visit."

Upon hearing the news, Chin Shee sank into a deeper depression, whereupon Lew Hing contacted the lawyers and asked them to continue to update him when court decisions were issued.

It was not until an 1890 case in the Federal District Court for the District of Oregon was there some inkling of how the courts might address this problem. In the first case involving the kind of documents merchants' wives must show upon arrival, Chung Toy Ho, the wife of Wong Ham, a well-known merchant in Portland, Oregon, returned with him to the United States after his visit to China. The couple brought their eight-year-old daughter, Wong Choy Sin, with them. Wong Ham had a "Section 6" certificate and was allowed to land upon arrival, but the collector denied admission to his wife and daughter, who had no separate certificates of their own. He based his decision on a ruling of the Treasury Department dated August 19, 1889 that stated that "the wife of a Chinese merchant who has never been in the United States cannot be allowed to enter the United States, with or without her husband, otherwise than upon the production of the certificate required by Section 6 of the act of July 5, 1884."[17]

In other words, members of the exempted class of the exclusion act must show a "Section 6 certificate" upon reentry into the United States. The merchant thought that by derivative application this would include spouse and children, but according to the interpretation of the immigration officer, any Chinese leaving the United States and seeking reentry must have their own "Section 6 certificate."

The matter went to court where Judge Matthew Deady of the circuit court for the District of Oregon who heard the case, decided that "the petitioners are not within the purview of the exclusion act of 1888 which is confined to laborers and that although they might conceivably be classed among

[17] 22 United States Statutes at Large 60; Act of July 5, 1884.

the "Chinese persons other than laborers" specified in the act of 1884, he did not think they were the "persons" legislators were referring to when they wrote that act. He pointed out that Chinese women were not usually teachers, students, or merchants, so it was not possible for them to obtain "Section 6" certificates. Moreover, the treaty of 1880 permitted Chinese merchants to bring their body and household servants with them, and if such persons could enter, surely wives and minor children had even greater right to do so. He therefore concluded that if merchants were entitled to come and enter the United States, so could their wives and children. The company of one, and the care and custody of the other, are his by natural right, and he ought not be deprived of either." He accordingly ordered Chung Toy Ho and her daughter to be released from custody even though they had no "Section 6" certificates of their own.

Although the *Chung Toy Ho* decision kept the door open for merchants' wives, it did not mean that no obstacles lay in their way. The United States did its best to try to restrict immigration by throwing up one hurdle after another.

One such hurdle was posed by Chinese marriage customs, the legality of which was called into question in the case of Lum Lin Ying, who had been betrothed to Chung Chew when she was only two years old. The actual marriage ceremony was performed in China when she reached the age of eighteen, with her would-be husband, by then an established merchant in Oregon, *in absentia.* Though Chung Chew did not return to China for the ceremony, he had consulted a team of lawyers in Portland. They drew up a document for him stating that the ceremony being performed in China formalized Chung Chew's and Lum Lin Ying's marital relationship. Chung then sent this "certificate" of his own making to his bride, asking her to bring it along with her to the United States as evidence that they were lawfully wedded husband and wife. But upon her arrival, the collector refused to allow her to land. She filed a writ of *habeas corpus* and took her case to the District Court for the District of Oregon.

Presiding Judge Charles B. Bellinger turned to the *Encyclopedia Britannica,* the only authority on Chinese marriage customs available to him, to read about the subject. Based on the information in the encyclopedia, he decided that the petitioner's marriage, as performed, was legal in China. He then observed that English and American legal doctrine held that a marriage which was valid in the place where it was contracted was valid everywhere. Therefore, in his view, the marriage under review was legitimate. However, he wondered, since the husband had remained in the United States during the ceremony, could it not be argued that the ritual had been solemnized in the United States, whereupon American custom should prevail? The good judge did not answer his own question but he decided that since the parties had acted with "the utmost good faith," and since Lum Ling Ying was neither a prostitute (as rumors had alleged her to be) nor a member of "any class of persons within the exclusion acts," it would be "a cruel injustice" to deny her entry. He therefore ordered her discharged from custody.[18]

In 1897, Mr. Riordon contacted Lew Hing with encouraging news: *"Mr. Lew, the right of merchants' wives to enter without certificates was affirmed by the Supreme Court. If and when you and/or your wife and family wish to travel to*

---

[18] Sucheng Chan, "The Exclusion of Chinese Women, 1870-1943." *Chinese Immigrants and American Law,* Volume 1, 1994, Garland Publishing, Inc., pp 114-118.

China and then return, we will prepare the necessary package of documents to facilitate reentry."

By this time, the family had grown. In addition to daughter Yuet-yung born in 1879 or 1880 and son, Lew Gin-gow, born in 1885, there was a daughter, Lew Yuen-hing born in 1889; a daughter, Lew Wai-hing born in 1890; a son, Lew Gun-sin born in 1894; a son Ming Lew (1896-1899); a son Lew Quay (1897-1905); and a daughter Lew Soon-hing. With such a large family of young children, Chin Shee didn't feel comfortable enduring the long voyage alone to China so she and Lew Hing decided to wait to travel back together at the first opportunity.

LAUNCHING A NEW VENTURE PACIFIC FRUIT PACKING COMPANY 1883-1888

By 1881, when Lew Hing's tin can business had outgrown the third floor at 715 Commercial, he leased space at 621 Jackson Street. Over time, the shop had enough business to require five employees, one being Ah Chew who was the foreman. Ah Chew had been an eager learner and soon he was teaching others the craft so that each can produced was perfectly air tight.

Pleased with the success of the operation, Lew Hing continued to harbor dreams of producing a product he could sell to the white consumers. His experience of running into cash flow problems when he was at 715 Commercial Street made him even more conservative with money. To save money, he continued to draw a salary for doing what he had done before at Hing Kee in addition to providing the same services for his tin shop without drawing a salary there.

He continued to meet regularly with Bellingall to discuss stocks and also to seek his advice. One day, Bellingall gave him what seemed to be backward advice. *"Hing, your dream is to sell canned food directly to the public. To do so, you must have, as much as possible, what is called a vertically integrated business model from the ground to the consumer. Right now, you know how to manufacture tin cans but do you know how to process the food which goes into the cans?"*

Hing was deep in thought in considering what Bellingall had said and responded," You are right! I need to work in a cannery where they process the food to learn how to prepare the food safely for canning."

Again, Bellingall would vouch for Hing. "I will contact an owner friend who owns a cannery and get you a job. Because you are Chinese, he will give you the lowest paid, dirtiest jobs and treat you like dirt. It will be your job, just like at the tin shop, to gain his trust and confidence."

And so, for five years, divided between working from the ground up at a white cannery for three years and two years experimenting at the tin shop, he labored to perfect his technique of canning a safe product. With the knowledge he learned from observing, through many instances of exploding cans and spoiled contents after storing them in series after series of batches, he slowly was able to perfect the technique of processing fruits and vegetables for canning by 1886.

As Lew Hing came closer to perfecting his canning technique, he began thinking about the final step in his plan to provide a product directly to the consumer, which was to find a location and find capital. In his darkened office at the tin shop, while contemplating how to round up initial capital to show that his new cannery was a serious start-up, Lew

Hing racked his brain to find a solution. He focused on finding investors but what could be an enticement to convince someone to invest in a new venture? Then, he recalled stories of fellow clansmen complaining about not being able to travel to China, whether for business or family because of the Exclusion Act. Surely there must be some unintended consequences of the Exclusion Act which might help—perhaps some loopholes?

The next day, he appeared in the offices of Reddy, Campbell and Metson, known to him as sympathetic to Chinese affairs.

"Mr. Lew, let's take a look at the law. The law is quite draconian as to laborers but might aid owners of particular businesses to qualify as merchants through a system of visa preferences. 'Merchant status' could enable persons to enter the United States, travel between the United States and China and sponsor relatives."

The attorney carefully outlined the law and Lew Hing asked a series of questions, only addressing the Merchant status. The attorney said that without speaking with the immigration officials as to specific requirements, it appears possible that a minimum investment and having white vendors who did business with the business testify as to the individual's role in the business might qualify for "Merchant" status.

Lew Hing was satisfied with the opinion and left the office to think about how to proceed.

The next day, he hired the firm to prepare an investment prospectus. Lew Hing put his plan in motion by inviting Sze Yup Lew clansmen to his tin shop for a presentation.

Most of the curious, drawn by the potential of unrestricted travel back and forth to China, listened intently as Lew Hing spoke.

"Fellow clansmen, as more and more of our Sze Yup brothers come to San Francisco looking for work, the only opportunities for them in Chinatown are with Sam Yup merchants who treat them poorly and we cannot do anything about it! In addition, the Exclusion Act has prevented those of you who wish to visit your families here, or to start businesses here with connections to China such as dry goods stores, are not able to do so. I have asked white attorneys to research how we might overcome this restriction. Let me introduce Mr. Reddy who will describe the investment document with me translating for you. After, I welcome questions from you."

The reception was lukewarm at first as the investment amount required to qualify as specified by the "Merchant" exception to the Exclusion Act was steep. However, the Chinese, for whom weighing odds was second nature, concluded that the potential reward outweighed the risk. The cannery project was oversubscribed.

In 1888, Lew Hing leased the entire four-story building at 804 Stockton Street, named the venture "Pacific Fruit Packing Company", capitalized at $50,000 with $2,000 to $3,000 of his own money and contributions of 38 partners, almost all fellow clansmen, most in San Francisco and America and some living in China, each with an interest of more than $500.

However, despite the $50,000 investment by the partners, they had no real interest in investing more, having achieved their objective. But Lew Hing knew from his prior ventures—Hing Kee and the tin shop—that cash flow was critical to the success of a new venture. He needed to find someone who could act as a banker when cash was needed to keep the operation running. Luckily, he had met the owner of another Sze Yup dry goods store, Lew Kan. Although Sze Yup, his ancestral roots were in Xinhui.

Seven years older than Lew Hing, Lew Kan came to America in 1866 at the age of 14 and was a self-made man; by 1868, he owned Lun Sing & Co. at 706 Sacramento Street, one of the earliest businesses in Chinatown. Lew Hing knew that Lew Kan was influential among the Sze Yup community, and he thought it would be good to establish a relationship with Lew Kan to work on mutually beneficial opportunities.

Lew Hing paid Lew Kan a visit at Lun Sing & Co. *"Honorable Lew Kan, permit me to introduce myself. I am Lew Hing, a partner in Hing Kee & Co. and owner of a tin shop making tin cans for canning salmon at 621 Jackson Street. I have 38 investors who have given me $50,000 to start a cannery for fruits and I have spent five years perfecting the process of preparing the food to be canned. I would like to know if you are interested in making loans in the event operating capital is needed. I am willing to pledge collateral for any loans I may need."*

Lew Kan stated, *"I will consider it if I can visit Hing Kee and your tin shop to see how these businesses are performing and you agree to show me the profit and loss statements for each business."*

Lew Hing replied, *"That is fair."*

PACIFIC FRUIT PACKING COMPANY OPENS FOR BUSINESS

1888

In 1888, Pacific Fruit Packing Company opened for business at 804 Stockton Street. Consistent with his goal of selling into the largest market and hoping to avoid anti-Chinese attention, Lew Hing realized that his ventures needed to be as "white" as possible, hence the name Pacific Fruit Packing Company. With his own business supplying the cans, he proceeded to hire a white firm, Minaker & Welbanks, to buy

Pacific Fruit Packing Co. at 804 Stockton, on right, next to Chinese Consulate

fruits and vegetables, and Frank H. Foote, a white merchandise broker as his sales agent to sell the products. They were marketed under three different brands: Pacific Fruit Packing

Company of San Francisco, San Francisco Fruit Canning Company and Alameda Canning & Packing Company.

The cannery property was leased from white owner, Joseph Goetz, who owned substantial property in Chinatown. As the one-time president of the 200-plus white property owners of the Chinatown Property Owner's Association, he would be instrumental in rallying the property owners to oppose the relocation of Chinatown after the 1906 earthquake.

The cannery was a success from the start and by 1889, Pacific Fruit Packing Co. expanded to 808 and 810, surrounding the Chinese consulate at 806 Stockton Street. Later, the cannery further expanded to 802 Stockton in 1892.

All the canning operations were conducted in the basement, which opened out onto an enclosed back area. In every building there was a hatch door and elevator through which crates of fruits were delivered from the street to the basement and finished canned products brought to the street level. Close to the hatch door in the basement were several long tables where about 30 to 40 white women and young girls busied themselves stoning peaches and cherries. Beyond that, and reaching the entire length of each room, were several long tables where dozens of Chinese worked elbow to elbow cutting fruits, packing them into cans, pouring in syrup, and putting on lids. After this was done, the cans were placed on trays and lowered by cranes into several gigantic kettles in the backyard to be boiled.

CONGRESS PASSES GEARY ACT EXTENDING EXCLUSION OF CHINESE

1892

When the 1882 Chinese Exclusion Act was due to expire in 1892, Congressman Thomas J. Geary of California introduced a new bill to extend the limitation on Chinese immigration to the United States. Based on the continued assumption that low-wage Chinese laborers were responsible for the economic downturn in the last quarter of the nineteenth century, particularly in California. Extending the immigration moratorium for an additional ten years, it was signed into law on May 5, 1892.

In an article published in 1893, titled *Should the Chinese Be Excluded*, the authors, Col. R.G. Ingersoll and Representative Geary, laid blame for the Geary Act at the feet of Chinese Six Companies.

> "If previous laws had been complied with this law would not be necessary. It is known from experience in California, where nine-tenths of all the Chinese in the United States reside that the great mass of Chinamen here would gladly and willingly have complied with the law but for the threats of their master, the Six Companies, who hold the great mass of Chinese in the United States under their control and authority....
>
> "There would have been no failure to comply with this law on the part of the Chinese but for the Six Companies, whose antagonism to it is not because of the degradation which it offers to their subjects, but for the reason that the enforcement of the law would insure a certain means of preventing in the future any further importation of their slaves. It

is the destruction of their slave industry that caused Six Companies to make the effort they have made to secure defeat of this law, and not any love for the vassals now in their employment here."[19]

No. 33880 ORIGINAL.

UNITED STATES OF AMERICA.

Certificate of Residence.

Issued to Chinese PERSON OTHER THAN LABORER, under the Provisions of the Act of May 5, 1892.

This is to Certify That Lew Hing, a Chinese PERSON OTHER THAN LABORER, now residing at SAN FRANCISCO, CALIFORNIA has made application No. 1280 to me for a Certificate of Residence, under the provisions of the Act of Congress approved May 5, 1892, and I certify that it appears from the affidavits of witnesses submitted with said application that said Lew Hing was within the limits of the United States at the time of the passage of said Act, and was then residing at SAN FRANCISCO, CALIFORNIA and that he was at that time lawfully entitled to remain in the United States, and that the following is a descriptive list of said Chinese PERSON OTHER THAN LABORER via:

Name: Lew Hing Age: 36 years

Local Residence: 801 ... St.

Occupation: ... Height: 5-7 in. Color of Eyes: Brown

Complexion: ... Physical Marks or Peculiarities for Identification: Scar on upper lip

And as a further means of identification, I have affixed hereto a photographic likeness of said Lew Hing.

Given under my hand and seal this second day of February 189.., San Francisco, State of CALIFORNIA

Collector of Internal Revenue, District of CALIFORNIA

Lew Hing's Certificate of Residence

The Geary Act also imposed a form of identity status on demand. All Chinese in the country were required to obtain official certificates of residence from the Internal Revenue Service, carry it at all times and produce it on demand. The punishment for failure to produce a certificate on demand was onerous: one year of hard labor followed by deportation. Bail was not permitted for immigrants arrested for being in the country "illegally" and only a "credible white witness" could testify on behalf of an accused. The Act was upheld by the U.S. Supreme Court in 1893 in Fong Yue Ting v. United States.

In 1894, Six Companies lost face and prestige in the Chinese community when its attempt to pressure the whole community to not register under the Act, as well as to donate one dollar to hire lawyers to fight for their rights, failed.

In 1902, Congress extended the Geary Act indefinitely.

---

[19] (Col. R.G. Ingersoll and Representative Geary of California, *Should the Chinese Be Excluded?*, North American Review, Volume 157, Issue 440, July 1893.

WHITES TARGET PACIFIC FRUIT PACKING COMPANY

1891-1893

Hiring white workers for the cannery was a conscious move by Lew Hing as he wanted to dispel the myth of mainstream cultural bias depicting Chinese as subservient, submissive and inferior to whites. However, the white press seized upon this arrangement, attempting to cast it in a negative light. The July 10, 1891 *San Francisco Chronicle* described the arrangement as "reversing things with a vengeance" and "rather startling." Seeking to stoke the flames of anti-Chinese sentiments, the article emphasized in particular the possible abuse of white women and girls working under Chinese bosses. The article was published even though the author knew the allegations were unsupported.

It took eight years before an out-of-town newspaper, *Stockton Evening Mail* on Monday, May 15, 1899, in a rare rebuke, pointed out the misleading nature of the Chronicle article.

"ONE SENSATION THAT FAILED"

> "Some years ago a San Francisco newspaper ascertained that Chinese canneries in that city employed a large number of white girls; and feeling pity for girls driven to accept employment from Chinamen, believing that gross abuses must be connected with such a system and also having a business-eye to the sensation that might be made by a slashing exposure of such a dreadful state of affairs, said newspaper sent reporters to view the factories and to hear the sad stories of the girls. They had no sad stories to tell, and the sensation did not materialize.

> They were found to be of a class superior to the ordinary run of cannery girls—better dressed, with a look of being better cared for, better in speech and demeanor, of a higher grade generally. They said they worked for the Chinese because they preferred to do so. They were better treated in every way. Proper accommodations were provided for them. In case of enforced absence by illness, or being taken ill at their work, they received consideration and kindness. Furthermore, they were 'never insulted.' They seemed to lay on that last point undue stress that was not complimentary to the white men who owned and managed the other canneries. In short, they convinced the reporters that any attempted sensation as to employment by Chinese would fall very flat and that they would help flatten it. So the scheme of exposing the employment of white girls by Chinese was dropped. It would have proved a boomerang and would have done the anti-Chinese cause no good at all…"

Still, the damage was done. The racist whites in San Francisco could not resist "tarring" Pacific Fruit Packing and Lew Hing with the "racist" brush. As one local newspaper lamented,

> "[I]n 1893, following the Supreme Court decision upholding the constitutionality of the Geary Act, a disgruntled ex-fruit canner was quoted as saying: 'The Chinese are ruining every business. They learn how to can fruit, and then lease a shed in which they and the slaves of the Six Companies go to work. The canner will take anything if it is cheap. A leper is able to solder cans, peel tomatoes, or remove the stones from plums and apricots. He is

> cheap and he is given work. You can go to a Chinese cannery on Stockton street today and buy canned fruit labeled "Made by white labor." You can buy shoes made in Chinatown factories that are put on the market as the product of white labor. You can buy cigars labeled "Key West" which have been made in Ross alley. In short, John Chinaman is the most dishonest man in the mercantile world. Drive him out of it and the poor American will be able to make a living for his wife and children. If the pagan stays he will own everything. He will live in a hole and have his work done by men who cost less for their keep than a good dog." [20]

These two articles, specifically targeting Pacific Fruit Packing Company, one attempting to portray Chinese as preying on white women and girls needing jobs, and the other a racist screed about a cannery on Stockton Street, exemplified without any doubt the increasing anti-Chinese fervor of the whites during the 1890s.

SOCIAL UNREST THREATENS STABILITY IN CHINATOWN

1895

In 1895, the anti-Chinese sentiment was matched only by the disdain in which the white government held the Chinese. Taking a hands-off approach to the squalid and overcrowded Chinatown, the Chinese essentially were left to self-govern, forming the Chinese Consolidated Benevolent Association also known as Six Companies. Originally organized in the

[20] *San Francisco Morning Call*, May 16, 1893, p. 7.

1850s but not formally established until 1882, it was composed of the six most important Chinese organizations in California at the time: Sam Yup, Yeung Wo, Kong Chow, Ning Yueng, Hop Wo and Yan Wo.

As the most powerful organization in Chinatown, Six Companies sought to thwart prostitution, encourage moral behavior and speak for the Chinese Community nationwide. Composed of wealthy merchants, it sought to use its political power, with the backing of the Chinese government, to protect the Chinese at a time when the United States unilaterally abrogated the Burlingame Treaty. Six Companies represented the Chinese in dealing with local, state and national governments on immigration and other issues.

From the moment they arrived in America, Chinese immigrants organized mutual aid societies which fell into three broad categories. The first type, regional societies, were set up by and for people from a specific district in Guangdong Province who spoke a common dialect. People who came from Taishan, who made up the majority of residents in Chinatown, spoke Sze Yup and generally belonged to the Ning Yeung Society. Those from the three counties nearer to Guangzhou or Canton, who spoke Sam Yup, were members of the Sam Yup Benevolent Association.

The second category were clan societies, membership available to Chinese from anywhere who shared a surname and were presumed to be kin. For example, the Wong or Lee Family Association or in the case of Lew Hing, the Four Family Association also known as Loong Kong Tien Yee composed of Lew, Quan, Jung and Chew surnamed individuals.

Membership in both the regional and clan organizations was near automatic and the dues were used to help new immigrants get settled, find housing and get established in business. The associations made loans to aspiring businessmen, provided bail and legal fees for the arrested, offered protection from harm and mediated disputes among their members.

The third category were the Tongs, sworn brotherhoods with no geographic or family requirements which existed in Chinatown from as early as 1854. Over the years, more and more Tongs were established, formed to protect their countrymen from discrimination by others as well as criminals in general.

However, criminal elements found the Tongs a useful vehicle as a way to participate in illicit activities, attempting to corner the market on activities such as prostitution, opium, gambling and extortion. Many Tongs hired salaried soldiers, known in Chinatown as "Boo How Doy" or hatchetmen. To the whites, they were known as "highbinders" because they would bind their queue on top of their heads to prevent themselves from being grabbed by an opponent.

The Six Companies battled the Tongs for nearly 50 years. While the Tongs were kept in check from the 1850s to 1870s, the economic pain and overcrowding, caused by anti-Chinese sentiment and pogrom of the mid-1870s to mid-1880s, challenged the ability of the Six Companies to maintain social order.

The Six Companies' control of Chinatown suffered a serious setback in 1894 when they were unable to rally the community to refuse to register as required by the Geary Act and to donate $1.00 to fight the Geary Act in courts. Taken as a sign that they were unable to effectively govern, the criminal element took center stage as Tong Wars erupted on the streets of Chinatown.

In addition to the violence in the streets, the Sze Yup seized on the Six Companies' loss of legitimacy as the governing body to organize a boycott of Sam Yup businesses. The Sze Yup protested the latter's monopolistic domination of certain types of Chinatown businesses, especially in the import-export area.

In 1895, fearful of being without protection in an increasingly lawless and bitterly divided Chinatown, Sam Yup merchants surnamed Lew, Quan, Jung and Chew sought to protect themselves by formally establishing the San Francisco Lodge of the worldwide clan organization, Loong Kong Tien Yee Association (commonly known as Four Family Association). At the same time, they established a separate organization, Mu Tin or Four Brothers, to protect members from unfair hostilities.

While membership was initially restricted by invitation only, Lew Hing, although Sze Yup, was invited to join, undoubtedly due to his ownership of the largest business in Chinatown and his close relationship with the Chinese consul. It was better to have him in rather than out. Lew Hing's membership with Four Family Association would be instrumental in funding his later investments.

A CALCULATED MARRIAGE

1898

In 1898, as their oldest daughter, Lew Yuet-yung reached marriage age, Lew Hing and Chin Shee set about to find a suitable husband. Chin Shee believed in the ancient practice of tossing fortune sticks as she had learned in Canton and brought with her to America. She stated her question and threw the sticks, question, answer, question, answer. She then told Lew Hing that the fortune sticks answered her with the following: *"He should be around twenty from a successful merchant family."*

Lew Hing launched a discreet campaign starting with the Four Family Association. Lew Hing's research showed a fellow member of the Quan clan, Quan Ying Nung who owned Gum Tong Tai. In existence since the 1850s when it was started by his father, Quan Shi Jiao, it was a well established wholesale supplier of dry goods from China.

Judge Milius King Harris, guardian of Quan Yeen

Moreover, Quan Ying Nung was fluent in both Chinese and English. Quan Ying Nung had three sons, Quan Poon, Quan Yeen and Quan Jwe. Of the three, Quan Yeen was nearing twenty and fluent in both Chinese and English. He had been sent to live in Fresno with a guardian, Judge Milius King Harris.

Lew Hing approached Quan Ying Nung, inviting him to tea. Deliberately choosing to speak English to minimize the differences in language (Sze Yup vs. Sam Yup) between them, he spoke: *"Thank you for honoring me with your presence."*

"I am pleased to have this opportunity to speak English," *Quan responded. "Only my son, Quan Yeen and I speak and read English so it is refreshing to be able to indulge my desire to speak with another in English."*

Lew Hing: "It is about your son, Quan Yeen that I wish to discuss with you...and his future if I may be so forward."

Quan Ying Nung: "I am always delighted to speak about my son's future."

The formalities addressed, Lew Hing said: "I am most grateful to you for speaking in support of my admission to Loong Kong."

Quan Ying Nung: "The Association is most honored to have one of the most successful merchants in the Chinese community and a stellar example of how a merchant can, at a time of great anti-Chinese sentiment, conduct commerce with whites."

Lew Hing: " The reason for this meeting is a family issue. I have decided to retire and go to China with my family. However, I have a dutiful daughter, raised by her mother to be a good wife and producer of children who is reaching marriage age. I would like to inquire of your son's future."

Quan Ying Nung: "I have a branch of my business in Fresno Chinatown and, when I moved my family back from Fresno to San Francisco, I left Quan Yeen in Fresno in the care of my white attorney to learn English, and American customs, for nine years. I brought him back to San Francisco to learn more Chinese with the intent to send him back in the future to run the business. There are no suitable candidates for him to marry there so I am delighted to share your suggestion with my wife."

Lew Hing: "May I suggest to my wife that she and my daughter can meet your wife?"

Quan Ying Nung: "I would be delighted to speak on behalf of my wife to such a meeting."

On January 2, 1898, Quan Yeen and Lew Yuet-yung married at the home of Quan Ying Nung at 7 Dupont Street. In attendance were Quan Yeen's guardians when he was young, Judge M. K. Harris and his wife and daughter, who traveled from Fresno for the occasion. The newlyweds then left for Fresno where Quan Yeen resumed control of the business interests.

WHITE CANNERS' COMBINE THREATENS EXISTENCE OF PACIFIC FRUIT PACKERS COMPANY

1899

While contending with being the target of anti-Chinese sentiment, a direct challenge to Lew Hing's cannery emerged in 1899. Eighteen of the pioneering white canners combined to form the California Fruit Canners Association (CFCA). The merger created an entity that represented 75 percent of the fruit canning capacity of the entire state. They formed a stock company with $3,500,000 capital on paper, but there was little coordination of CFCA operations. Rather than creating a centralized company, the CFCA was more an alliance of former competitors. The original canners enjoyed high levels of independence for newly merged companies. Canneries continued to pack under existing brand names, but they did cooperate via packaging under a common brand, Del Monte.

Even before formally forming CFCA, the white canners had locked up all the East and South Bay orchards, forcing Pacific Fruit to incur more transportation cost in sourcing from Sacramento and as far north as Chico. They then joined together to use buying power to obtain cheaper freight, supply and fruit costs. With superior purchasing power, they were able to force growers to accept their price for perishable products or resort to drying the fruit.

CFCA attempted to use its superior purchasing power to undercut and drive independent canners, both white and Chinese, out of business. For example, the cartel forced the growers to accept no more than 3/4 to 1 cent per pound for premium apricots or peaches while Pacific Fruit paid 1-1/2 to 1-3/4 cents per pound for inferior quality apricots and peaches. If Pacific Fruit wanted premium raw materials, it had to source from farms and ranches from Sacramento and as far north as Chico, increasing transportation costs.

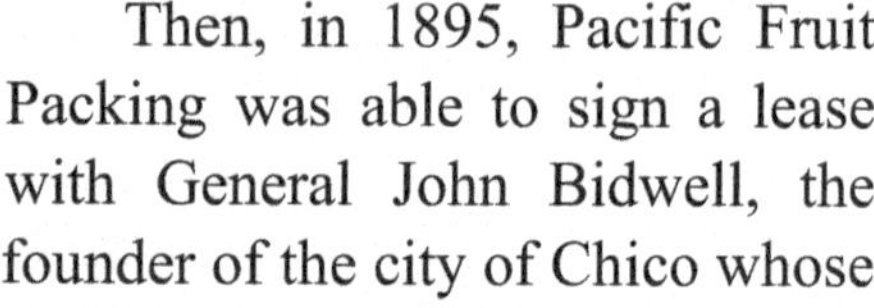

Quan Yeen at Winters Ranch

As the combine continued its campaign to eliminate competition, Lew Hing sought ways to stay competitive. In 1893, Pacific Fruit Packing (PFP) purchased 80 acres of the thousands of acres of the Wolfskill Ranch in Winters, California, paying $500 per acre or $40,000 for land which produced premium early cherries, apricots, peaches, and plums in great abundance each year.

Then, in 1895, Pacific Fruit Packing was able to sign a lease with General John Bidwell, the founder of the city of Chico whose enormous Rancho Chico with over 95,000 fruit trees was said to be the largest in the world. The lease was all encompassing. Lew Hing's army of hundreds of laborers would be sent to Bidwell's ranch to prepare the fruit trees and to pick the fruits when ripe. Undoubtedly, this is where Lew Kan helped Lew Hing survive by extending credit when the cartel thought they could financially squeeze him out of business.

To save transport costs in hauling fruits, PFP entered into an exclusive contract with the Canton Express owned by a Chinese man, Frank Dunn, rather than hiring any of the three white-owned drayage companies then operating in Chinatown. Both the use of laborers in the fields and using the Canton Express further antagonized and frustrated the combine.

Finally, Lew Hing had to resort to several cost-cutting measures, chief among them being to use Chinese in all skilled- or semi-skilled positions at wages much lower than whites could earn at their canneries. The lower wages for Chinese labor was probably the biggest reason why the company managed to stay in business.

THE PLAGUE THREAT

1900

The new century began with the discovery of the Bubonic plague in San Francisco. When the Bubonic Plague erupted in San Francisco, as in the 1850s and 1870s and 1880s, proposals to quarter the Chinese outside of the city limits of San Francisco were advanced. However, no formal condemnation proceedings were ever instituted and Chinatown remained located in the center of San Francisco. This central location brought the Chinese into daily contact with the Caucasian population of the city, a constant source of irritation to many San Franciscans. To one health officer, "Chinatown was 'the moral purgatory' through which all who pass come out nauseated and disgusted, and perchance defiled by Mongolian filth or disease."[21]

---

[21] *"Report of Special Committee on the Condition of the Chinese Quarter,"* Municipal Reports, 1885, p.208.

Lew Hing was in his offices on the second floor of the cannery on Stockton Street when a member of his office staff rushed in with upsetting news: *"Sir, the white authorities have announced the death of a countryman suspected of being the victim of the bubonic plague. We must take every precaution to protect our workers."*

Lew Hing calmly responded, "I already gave orders to the superintendent a week ago to start cleaning every part of the factory."

The week before, he had read an article in the local newspaper describing the appearance of the bubonic plague in Honolulu Chinatown. It caused him to think that a ship stopping in Honolulu on its way from Asia to the West Coast. might bring the plague to San Francisco. The article also told of authorities sealing off the area with the military and burning the affected buildings to contain the disease. Given the continued anti-Chinese sentiment, he could not discount the whites using the plague as a reason to burn Chinatown, including his cannery, to the ground thereby displacing the community as they had threatened to do before.

Once he knew that the *Nippon Maru*, which was the vessel suspected of carrying the diseased rats with infected fleas, had also arrived in Seattle with more dead crew and was bound for San Francisco, a sense of dread permeated his mind. But it wasn't just the *Nippon Maru* that came into the Port of San Francisco in January, 1900. A four-masted steamship *S. S. Australia,* which sailed regularly between Honolulu and San Francisco, laid anchor around the same time as the *Nippon Maru*. Although its passengers and crew were declared clean, authorities suspected that cargo from Honolulu unloaded at the docks near the outfall of the Chinatown sewers may have allowed rats carrying the plague to leave the ship and transmit the infection. Wherever it came from, the disease soon established itself in Chinatown when a sudden increase in dead rats was observed as the infections spread.

The first death was of a bachelor, Wong Chut King, aka

Barbed-wire barricade around Chinatown, 1899, from *The Wave*, Issue No. 21, Jan-July 1900.

Chick Gin or Wing Chung Gin. He was single and lived in the basement of the Globe Hotel, a once fancy building in the style of an Italian palazzo built in 1857, but now a squalid tenement crowded with Chinese bachelors. Falling ill on February 7, 1900 with what the doctors thought was typhus or gonorrhea, he became gravely ill as the medications failed. Passing away after four weeks, he was taken to the Chinese undertaker where the body was examined by the San Francisco police surgeon, Frank Wilson, on March 6, 1900. Finding symptoms associated with the plague—swollen glands—the surgeon called a city health official named O'Brien who summoned Kellogg, the city bacteriologist, and the three performed an autopsy, discovering plague bacilli.

Noise from the street in front of his residence on the fourth floor at 804 Stockton Street interrupted Lew Hing's morning reading of the newspaper. He went quickly to the window to discover what was inevitable since he first learned of the plague in Honolulu: Chinatown was quarantined. Looking out the window, he saw a rope running up and down the street and police stationed to prevent egress or access to anyone but whites. He hurriedly dressed and walked next door to the Chinese consulate where he found people standing on the porch, including Consul Ho, who told him of the death of Wong Chut King, which was the name used by the public health official to identify the deceased to the Consul General.

"Lew Hing, I wish I could say it is a good morning but as you can see, we have a problem."

"Consul Ho, while you have made a good impression with the whites, now we will see the true attitude of the whites towards us. Having been here since 1869 and witnessed many incidents of anti-Chinese sentiment and violence, I am not surprised with their heavy-handed approach. You are in for a rough time dealing with the white authorities," Lew Hing replied.

"Come walk with me and my staff as we try to calm the crowds of our countrymen."

They first walked along the roped section of the twelve-block area bounded by Stockton, Broadway, Kearney and California Streets before turning onto Dupont Street via Commercial Street from Kearney. A large number of the 15,000 residents packed into the ghetto were out on the streets at the time. Lew Hing and Consul Ho and the staff of the Consulate were encircled at every turn, trying to answer questions and reduce the anxiety of the residents.

That afternoon, Consul Ho convened a meeting of the Six Companies, seeking their advice and preparing a community response to the white officials. He got an earful. Those who had witnessed the reaction of the whites during the 1876 smallpox plague spoke of the widespread racism towards Chinese immigrants, and how Chinatown was blamed as being the locus of unsanitary and decrepit conditions, ignoring the fact that American landlords refused to maintain their own property when renting to Chinese immigrants. The living conditions in Chinatown were neither fit nor adequate for human living, but with scarce housing options and white landlords unwilling to provide equal and fair housing, Chinese immigrants were left little option but to live in squalor and unsanitary conditions, conditions conducive to diseases.

At the same time while blaming the Chinese, San Francisco public officials had denied group access to health care, refusing to finance critical services in Chinatown and raising the cost of treatment for Chinese patients at municipal hospitals.

At the meeting, the wealthy merchants agreed that the community must immediately address the need for a hospital to minimize the potential spread of the infection. Lew Hing, president of both the Pacific Fruit Packing Company and Hop Wo Lung Dry Goods, made a sizable contribution toward the building of the first Chinese-owned hospital in America, Tung Wah Dispensary.

Consul Ho had promised the residents and assured the merchants that he would seek a court order lifting the quarantine but faced a court not inclined to be sympathetic to their position, as then-Mayor Phelan was in favor of keeping the Chinese separate from the whites, claiming that the Chinese were unclean, filthy and "a constant menace to the public health."

Despite these pronouncements, inexplicably, on March 9, the Board of Public Health lifted the quarantine. It may have been due to the fact that animals exposed to the plague-causing agents seemed normal after 48 hours, casting doubt at that time on the cause of Wong's death.

Without restoring the quarantine that caused such an uproar, the Board of Health inspected every building in Chinatown in an attempt to disinfect the neighborhood. Property was seized and burned if it was suspected of harboring filth, with the police using physical violence to enforce the Board of Health directives.

Lew Hing was concerned about the edict of the city officials. It would be catastrophic to the business. Even more troubling was the potential of a jealous white competitor or racist claiming that the infection originated at one of the buildings which might cause the public officials to order the buildings burned to the ground.

Lew Hing proactively put into action procedures to clean and sanitize the buildings and to screen his workers once he read about the Honolulu Chinatown incident. If rats were found and caught, he made sure they were killed and at a distance, carefully bagged and registered with the Rat Center set up by the public health officials. He also openly welcomed public health officials to investigate the cannery.

In the event white competitors might use this opportunity to eliminate Pacific Fruit, Lew Hing was prepared to convert the investor-based company into a stock corporation owned by him and his white partners—the land owner, the manager of operations, the commission agent and the company attorney. It would give the business a fighting chance to stave off any subterfuge by a competitor pandering to the anti-Chinese sentiment of the city officials. Fortunately, the cannery passed inspection and continued to operate. However, it would succumb to another threat, the white canners association.

WHITE COMPETITION DRIVES LEW HING OUT OF THE CANNERY BUSINESS

1902

"Turmoil followed industrialization in the American economy of the 1890s, the food industry included. The depression and rock bottom wages of the era led to poor sales and 'overproduction.' Competition among small growers and distributors destroyed many. Small canners, always pressed to meet loan payments or pay their workers, often unloaded their whole pack in the weeks following a harvest. Successful canners moved to reduce competition through consolidation.

Consolidation had swept other industries as well. The west coast fish packing industry concentrated itself in the Alaska Packers Association in 1893. Griffin & Skelley had grown into the largest packer in Southern California. Brothers J.K. Jr. and George Armsby led the formation of the Central California Canneries in 1901 and became the West's largest preserved foods distributors. Though these companies operated facilities all over the West, each maintained headquarters within a block of each other on Lower California Street in San Francisco."[22]

In 1902, weary of the continual stress of running the cannery and pressured by Chin Shee for him to devote more time to his family, Lew Hing sold Pacific Fruit Packing

[22] Chris Carlsson, *Del Monte Foods: Historical Essay*, internet source: foundsf.org., 2020.

Company to the very competitor which had been trying to drive him out of business, California Fruit Canners Association. He threw in the towel and vowed to leave the United States permanently, tired of the racial abuse. Even when he and his family departed for China, a local newspaper took a farewell shot at him, "Lew Hing, a Chinese proprietor of the Pacific Fruit Packing Company in the city, who fills the anomalous position of being the only Chinese who employs white girls in his business, sailed with his wife and children for a visit to China. In his factory Lew Hing employs about *(illegible)* white girls."[23]

THE REALITY OF CHINA HITS HOME
1902 – 1903

Lew Hing herded wife No. 1, Chin Shee, accompanied by their oldest daughter, Yuet-yung, her husband Quan Yeen and their first born, Anna (born in 1899 in San Francisco), and sons Lew Gin-gow, Lew Gun-sing, and daughters Lew Yuen-hing, Lew Wai-hing and Lew Soon-hing; and wife No. 2, Jung Loy, and son Quay aboard a Pacific Mail Steamship for Hong Kong in 1902.

He had been back to China only once since arriving in America, for a short trip beginning in 1894 to visit family in Canton and to set up a general merchandising export company, Hop Wo Chong in Hong Kong. During his brief stay in Canton, he also married a young woman, Jung Loy, only 18 at the time. He and his wife No. 2 returned in June of 1894 to San Francisco where he intended to open a general merchandising store Hop Wo Lung in San Francisco. In 1895, he invested first $2,000 and eventually $30,000 in Hop Wo Lung.

---

[23] *San Francisco Chronicle*, February 26, 1902.

When Lew Hing and his whole family returned to China this time, it was to establish their home permanently in Canton. Lew Hing had purchased a large home on Fung Yuan Nam which featured an enclosed courtyard large enough to hold four sedan-chairs. In a fashionable section of Canton, the house was a building flanked by two buildings of two stories with balconies where the servants were housed. There was a special room for opium smoking.

At Lew Hing's house in Canton, China with daughter Yuet-yung and relatives in courtyard

When Lew Hing and his family arrived in Canton, he was welcomed like a conquering hero, having overcome the racism and violence of white America to be enormously successful. He still maintained his contact with San Francisco Chinatown as Hop Wo Chong in Hong Kong continued to supply Hop Wo Lung. Lew Hing hoped that the money he received from the sale of Pacific Fruit Packing Company would fund new profit-making ventures in China. He turned to extended family members to help him invest.

However, the family stay in Canton was not pleasant for Lew Hing. He relied on family and distant relatives for businesses to invest as he was "like a fish out of water" about the business environment in China and Hong Kong. In 1902, he invested 2,000 yuan in Fook Heng, a silk and fabric business. Later in that year, he also invested in a pharmacy, Wuet Lun Dispensary. By early 1903, Lew Hing invested 1,000 taels (silver) in Lai Hing, a finance company. Then, in the same year, he invested 1,500 taels in Liu Wah Cheung, a fabric and clothing business. He also made a minor investment in a dried seafood business in Hong Kong, Heng Tai.

All of these businesses were short-lived as his relatives did not exhibit the same business prowess. Lew Hing would have preferred to remain retired, but running out of money, he had no choice but to return to America to start over once again.

FOUR

RETURN TO AMERICA 1903 - 1906

PLANNING A NEW CANNERY IN OAKLAND 1903

Lew Hing returned to America in 1903 with wife No. 1, Chin Shee, sons Gin-gow and "Tom" (Gunn-sing), and daughter "Rose" (Soon-hing). Daughters Yuen-hing and Wai-hing, being of marriageable age, remained in China to have husbands found for them. Wife No. 2, Jung Loy, also remained in China, where her son Quay was to be educated; unfortunately, both of them died there of illness within a few years.

In San Francisco, Lew Hing found a new home for his family on the south side of Sacramento Street between Kearney and Grant Avenue. Their last child, a son, Ralph, was born in 1903.

Having settled his family, Lew Hing turned to planning his next business. He surveyed the business landscape and realized he really only had expertise with canning fruits and vegetables. However, he also knew that competing with the behemoth, the California Fruit Growers Association, would make any venture challenging. The question in his mind was whether he could successfully start another cannery and how he could finance such a venture.

In planning a new cannery, Lew Hing must have carefully analyzed the trend in the fruit and vegetable canning industry and what he concluded can be summed up by a dissertation abstract for a PhD by Stephanie Esther Fuglaar Statz in December, 2012 titled *California's Fruit Cocktail: A History of Industrial Food Production, the State, and the Environment in Northern California*, in the early twentieth century:

> "The growing power of the canneries' production network was most visible in cities where the fruit canning industry consolidated. San Jose, Oakland and Modesto had higher concentrations, and the operations located with them were significantly larger than other canneries in California. Smaller canneries were scattered across the valleys, often in combination with nearby orchards and packing facilities, but these operations when taken together, rarely produced the same quantity of products as the large urban canneries nor exerted the same degree of power over the industry. Given their tremendous production capacity and their prominence in local economies, these large urban-based canneries exercised significant influence over the municipal governments in San Jose, Oakland and Modesto as well.
>
> "There were many advantages to building a cannery in a city in the late nineteenth and early twentieth century. Transportation was a decisive

factor in determining a cannery's location. The raw fruit that went into the canneries and packages of canned goods that emerged were quite heavy. Companies decreased shipping costs by finding a location near a railroad or port. The transcontinental railroad was completed by 1870; however, canners continued to rely on ocean transport for long-distance hauling for many years because it remained more affordable. During the fruit canning season, which ran from March to October, the canneries hired thousands of workers and urban centers tended to provide a more reliable labor force.

"In addition to reliable transportation and a steady supply of seasonal workers, canneries also required a large, consistent supply of water and an economical way to dispose of the many tons of waste produced during the canning season. It cost less for canneries to connect to existing water systems than to create their own...The seasonal pack required a huge volume of water for washing away the detritus from the fruit preparation process and operating machinery such as boilers and retorts. Cities constructed water systems that provided clean drinking water and enough pressure for fire hydrants. Fire was another major concern in quickly growing cities because wooden buildings outnumbered those made of brick or stone. In fact, fire was a constant worry in canneries before brick and concrete became more affordable and thus the industry's construction norm....Oakland's location

> and the fact that it hosted a railroad terminus connecting it to the transcontinental Railroad were vital in its growth."[24]

With the advent of the newly constructed rail system connecting the west, Lew Hing realized that there was a rapidly reachable and growing market for canned goods. So, his first move was to look for a site near rail lines which could move his product to faraway markets. He found the perfect location in the industrial area of Oakland, a mostly vacant area called West Oakland. If he could acquire the land, a large cannery could be built with a direct rail spur from the factory to the main rail line to the rest of the country.

Seeking to quickly acquire the land, he incorporated Pacific Coast Cannery in December, 1903, selling shares to fellow countrymen to raise the cash. With the money, Lew Hing began land acquisition through W.A. Richardson, his long-standing attorney, because Lew Hing, as an alien, was ineligible for naturalization under federal law.[25] As such, he could not own land in California as its law limited ownership only to whites and African Americans.[26]

Lew Hing still needed money to build the cannery and furnish it with the latest equipment. No banks would loan

---

[24] Statz, Stephanie Ester Fuglaar, California's Fruit Cocktail: A History of Industrial Food Production, the State and the Environment in Northern California, PhD Dissertation Abstract, University of Houston (December 2012) p.85-87 (uh-ir.tdl.org)

[25] United States 1870 Naturalization Act expanded the list of those eligible for naturalization to include all white persons and persons of African descent. Congress specifically rejected a proposal to open naturalization to all, including Chinese.

[26] In 1879, the California legislature revised the California constitution to limit the ownership of land to aliens who are of "the white race or of African American descent."

money to him because he was Chinese. He needed an intermediary with credibility to intercede with funding sources.

If he could find a white commission agency to help him secure a construction and equipment loan, he would offer that company an attractive deal. Fortunately, just three years prior, in 1900, an ambitious young man, James Rolph, had established the James Rolph Company, commissioned agents, giving the responsibility of operating the business to his brother, William Rolph.

Lew Hing believed he could interest the Rolphs in the business proposition he could offer. Lew Hing sent a letter to William Rolph requesting a meeting.

Dear Mr. Rolph:

I was the founder and General Manager of Pacific Fruit Packing Company here in San Francisco. It was a successful business from 1888 to 1902 when I sold it.
I am planning a new cannery and would like to discuss a possible business relationship with your company to commence in 1905. Might your company be interested in our business? If so, I am available to meet with you to discuss this matter.

Very Truly Yours,
Lew Hing

Lew Hing prepared himself for his new role in the white world of business. He cut his queue and trimmed his hair western style, grew a moustache and finally, purchased the most fashionable western business suit and a bowler hat. Unusually large for a Chinese man, Lew Hing, except for his face, could be mistaken for a white businessman.

Entering the Rolph offices and speaking impeccable English without an accent, he asked for William Rolph. Ushered into Rolph's office, William Rolph came from behind his desk, shook Lew Hing's hand and invited him to sit down. They exchanged pleasantries and Rolph explained he had known of Pacific Fruit Packing Company and its reputation for producing quality goods.

"Thank you for seeing me," Lew began.

"The pleasure is mine," Rolph responded, "How may I be of assistance?"

"I am planning to build a cannery, one city block in size next to the Southern Pacific Railhead in Oakland. It will be operational in 1905 and with rail access, I intend to distribute my product through the United States," Lew replied. " I am interested to know if your company would have the capacity to handle our account. I envision a much larger enterprise for the future as California and the United States present a huge untapped market. If I may, for a reference, please feel free to contact P.W. Bellingall at Bellingall Customs Brokers."

Upon hearing of potential for new business, Rolph concluded: "Let me give this some thought and discuss this my brother James and then we can get back with you."

The Rolphs discussed the matter among themselves, eventually speaking, as Lew Hing knew, with P.W. Bellingall. They concluded that Lew Hing was real and that the dealing with Lew Hing was a real opportunity for great rewards.

At a follow-up meeting with William Rolph, Lew Hing proposed the following, *"Mr. Rolph, instead of simply being the commissioned agents for the new cannery, I propose an arrangement between your company and the new cannery. That is, if we build the cannery together, I'm in charge of production and you're in charge of distribution and sales, we can more efficiently attack the market."*

There ensued more meetings, culminating in an agreement of Rolph helping find financing for the building and other services in exchange for exclusive rights to distribute the products and a higher commission on the sales. They also agreed that Lew Hing would have use of a desk at Rolph Company to better coordinate the activities of the new cannery.

James Rolph, c. 1912

For Lew Hing, a relationship with James Rolph Company was not just business—he was even more interested in the possibilities of a relationship with the politician, James Rolph.

James Rolph, who would serve as Mayor of San Francisco from 1912 to 1931, was born 11 years after Lew Hing in San Francisco. After graduating from Trinity School in 1888, he worked first in a commission agency and then for DeWitt, Kittle & Co. where he learned the shipping business.

Ambitious, he formed a shipping company, Hind & Rolph, with a former classmate from Trinity, George Hind, in 1900, as well as James Rolph Company, a commission agency for his brother William Rolph to run. In 1903, he helped found the Mission Bank. His later companies would include Rolph Shipbuilding Company and Rolph Navigation and Coal. He also would serve as president of the Shipbuilders Association of the Pacific Coast for three terms, President of the Merchants Exchange for three years and as a trustee of the Chamber of Commerce. All these businesses and organizations would eventually garner him the support to be considered mayoral material.

Rolph would later burnish his reputation in the aftermath of the 1906 earthquake by establishing the Mission Relief Agency of the Red Cross. His barn at 25th and Guerrero Streets became the headquarters for distributing food and supplies unloaded at the Southern Pacific station on nearby Valencia Street. Using his personal funds to feed thousands of displaced citizens there for a number of months, he engendered widespread admiration and support from the populace.

Lew Hing incorporated Pacific Coast Cannery in 1903 as an "open stock" corporation but did not openly offer shares to the public, instead offering shares to clansmen and whites he had known from his other cannery. However, he needed money to construct the new cannery.

To fund the venture, a loan was secured by the Rolph/Lew partnership from Donohoe-Kelly Banking Company. However, Lew Hing was not keen on continued reliance on a lender for cash when needed for operations.

The whites still did not trust Lew Hing nor did he trust them. Bertram Adams, who represented the Donohoe-Kelly Banking (DKB) company was at the site every day. And even after the cannery commenced operation, Adams was on site daily. However, he and Lew Hing seemed to co-exist as Adams actually vouched for Lew Chuck Suey, a fellow clansman of Lew Hing and an early business partner in Pacific Fruit Packing Company when he applied for "merchant status." PCCC paid for his presence from the advent of the loan until at least 1917 when the loan was paid off.

SEPARATING BUSINESS FROM FAMILY

Although Lew Hing was elated with the arrangement to fund his cannery, the white oversight prevented him from drawing excessive amounts of money from the new cannery to support his family, in particular, his sons who were now leading a profligate lifestyle. With a large family to support, he needed to find additional sources of money. Still maintaining interests in Hing Kee and Hop Wo Lung in Chinatown, he fully participated in the affairs of the family association upon his return to San Francisco.

Following up on the Chinatown response to the Bubonic plague which showed the need of the community to build a hospital, Lew Hing conceived the idea of the family association setting up a public welfare fund. With such a fund, not only could he enhance his reputation as a philanthropist but also skim money to support his family.

He arranged for a presentation at the formal meeting of the heads of the four families, each surname family represented by both a Sam Yup merchant and Sze Yup merchant, a modification of the governing structure to help with the unification of the association after the brutal disagreements of the Sam Yup and Sze Yup factions in Chinatown during the last decade of the nineteenth century.

He appeared in his capacity representing the Sze Yup Lew clan.

"Whether we are a Lew from Sam Yup or a Lew from Sze Yup," as he nodded respectfully across the table towards his Sam Yup counterpart, "we are surnamed Lew, brothers sharing the common ancestral name, the same with Quan, Jung and Chew. Loyalty to Loong Kong is in my mind paramount, regardless of which area one was from in China. That because of wars, famines and other causes, your ancestors migrated to the Sam Yup area and mine to the Sze Yup area many moons ago, should we allow where we are now from to divide us today?"

Lew Hing paused, and looked across the table at the Sam Yup representatives—he saw nearly unanimous nodding before continuing. "Because of the attitude of the whites towards us, whether Sam Yup or Sze Yup, it makes no difference to them, they do not like us and want to force us out. We individually make a donation each new year to help the less fortunate of our brothers. I propose, in addition, we establish a public welfare fund to more fully help brothers in need but to also contribute to community activities such as hiring attorneys to fight the discriminatory laws, to build community institutions like the Tung Wah Dispensary we donated to in 1900 and for other activities as we vote to deem for the benefit of all Chinese.

"Where does the money for the fund come from? Well, our brothers indulge in recreational activities, which we are all aware of. Why shouldn't we provide a safe place for them to enjoy these activities? We know the whites condemn such activities but still they condone them by allowing them to exist. The corrupt police are pleased to accept protection money to look the other way. We have Mu Tin which will defend our members who are unfairly treated, why shouldn't we use it to oversee these activities?"

The representatives debated the proposal before giving approval to establishing the fund and directing Lew Hing to return with the details at the next meeting. With the approval in hand, he then asked his old friend and former partner in Hing Kee, Lew Yu, to help him out one last time. Lew Hing then detailed his plan and asked Lew Yu to present it to the elders.

At the next meeting, Lew Yu, well known to all the merchants around the table as the successful owner of Hing Kee, made his presentation. At the conclusion of his presentation, Lew Hing rose to add his comments.

"I strongly suggest our association only be involved in gambling and opium, not brothels. My opposition to brothels is due to having three daughters so my opposition is personal. I would never condone having a young girl kidnapped or sold into sex slavery. And for more practical reasons, it would be counterproductive to the reputation of our Association to be involved in such activities when both Six Companies and the Consul General were attempting to stamp out the brothels. And perhaps on a more practical level, it isn't worth the trouble of tangling with the Tongs who have virtual control of that vice."

But Lew Hing would later turn a blind eye when Yuet-yung, his daughter, decided to use sex to help fill the seats at the Chinese opera. Visiting Chinese opera troupes were granted visitors visas as an exception to the Chinese Exclusion Act. Most roles, even female roles, were played by male actors but the troupes which came had many women assistants whose role really was to provide additional entertainment for the mainly male patrons. Of course, Yuet-yung shared in the profits from the services provided by the "assistants."

In regard to gambling, the lottery was the most popular. Players purchased randomly assigned sweepstakes numbers from gambling houses with drawings held at least once a day in lottery saloons. Such saloons would receive protection from corrupt police in exchange for weekly payoffs of a few dollars a week. This was the money maker. For opium, the whites were concerned about opium dens even though the importation and consumption of opium long predated Chinese immigration to the United States. But it was also a money maker.

In San Francisco, by 1876, there were 200 opium dens, each with a capacity of between five to fifteen people. But after the Burlingame Commercial Treaty of 1868, only American citizens could legally import opium into the United States, creating a black market for the importation of opium among the Chinese.

Chinatown Opium Den, c. 1890

In the early decades of the twentieth century, anti-Chinese advocates believed America faced a dual dilemma: opium smoking was ruining moral standards and Chinese labor was lowering wages and taking jobs away from whites. This perception of the Chinese continued to fan the flames of racism.

Despite the perception, white society continued to limit employment opportunities for Chinese, and condone illegal activities in Chinatown. As the funds flowed in to the public welfare fund, Lew Hing told the other elders at Loong Kong that he would keep the books and cash in his vault at the cannery as it was safer there than in Chinatown, and the alternative, putting it in a white bank, might raise suspicion as to its origins.

THE CROWN JEWEL OF HIS EMPIRE

1904

In 1904, with the DKB loan, Pacific Coast Cannery quickly took shape. The site, an entire city block, was located at the West Oakland waterfront adjacent to the Southern Pacific tracks bounded by Pine Street on the east and 12th street on the south and 13th street on the north.

Taking the ferry every day from San Francisco to Oakland in the morning to oversee the construction of the cannery, Lew Hing traveled with his bodyguard, both carrying business valises, ostensibly working papers related to the

Pacific Coast Cannery, West Oakland, 1905

construction. In reality, it was cash gathered by Lew Yu and Mu Tin members the night before, which was deposited in the large vault in the office.

Buckskin Brand label

In the spring of 1905, the cannery opened and by the summer, 300 girls and women were employed during the canning season. The new cannery produced canned fruits and vegetables under the "Buckskin Brand" label featuring a picture of a cowboy. Products included asparagus, cherries, apricots, peaches, pears, grapes and tomatoes.

Other than Lew Hing as the President, the officers and members of the board of directors were white: W. Woolbeck as Vice President, B.W. Bellingall as Secretary, and W. Manaker as Treasurer as well as a board composed of Lew Hing, P.W. Bellingall, W.A. Richardson, W. Manaker and W. Woolbeck, effectively hiding the fact that the cannery was a Chinese enterprise.

In August 1990, in an historical architecture report for the City of Oakland, Pacific Coast Canning Co. was described as follows:

> "111-99 Pine Street, the Pacific Coast Canning Co. is an early 20th century utilitarian cannery built in several phases. It is situated on a large, two-block-long site bordered by Pine Street on the east, the tracks and yard of the Southern Pacific Railroad on the west, 11th Street on the south and the vacated right-of way of 13th Street on the north. There is a continuous loading dock on the west and loading bays on the south, both originally served by spur tracks. The site is surrounded by industrial properties to the south, east and north.

"The property comprises four adjoining structures built between 1909 and c. 1928 to house the diverse functions of a fruit and vegetable cannery. From south to north, these sections are: (A) a reinforced concrete warehouse and cold storage building (1913); (B) a brick warehouse (1928; incorporating a 1909 structure); (C) a steel-frame cooling room (c. 1928); (D) a reinforced concrete cannery building (1919-1920)…

"1111-19 Pine Street, the Pacific Coast Canning Co., was an early and important Oakland plant established by Chinese-American industrialist Lew Hing. Lew Hing (b. 1857), a native of Canton, China, came to California in 1871, settling in San Francisco and moving to Oakland after the 1906 earthquake and fire. He became a leader in the Bay Area's canning industry, as well as developing banking and shipping interests in the Chinese community. In the 1880s he established a small cannery in San Francisco, the Pacific Fruit Packing Co., which he later sold. In 1903 -04, he organized the Pacific Coast Canning Co. in Oakland with a capital stock of $50,000. The company canned many varieties of fruits and vegetables—peaches, pears, apricots, cherries, grapes, asparagus, tomatoes—which it sold under the brand name "Buckskin." Lew Hing's cannery was a major employer of Chinese, Portuguese and Italians in West Oakland; as early as 1905, the company had 300 employees, and by 1911 it was one of Oakland's largest businesses, with 1,000 employees at peak season (mostly women). By 1914, according to Davis' Commercial

Encyclopedia, it was the third largest canning company on the West Coast.

"The Pacific Coast Canning Co. played an important role in the food processing and packaging industry that developed in California in the decades after 1880.

"It competed directly with such industry leaders as the California Packing Corporation (Del Monte). Although Lew Hing was not unique as a Chinese-born owner of a major cannery (Chin Hing, H.P. Chan and others built a $1 million plant for the Western Canning Co. in Emeryville in 1919, and in the South Bay there was the Bay Side Cannery of the Chew family), he is notable for his longevity of ownership and for his prominent role in the Bay Area's Chinese community."[27]

---

[27] Historical Architecture Survey Report Part VII. A, Subarea A: City of Oakland. *August 1990. Prepared by Staff and Consultants, Oakland Cultural Heritage Survey, Gary Knecht, Survey Coordinator, Oakland City Planning Department for CALTRANS District 4.*

FIVE

MAJOR BUSINESS SUCCESS

THE GREAT SAN FRANCISCO EARTHQUAKE 1906

At 5:13 a.m. on April 18, 1906, while the rest of his family was still in China, Lew Hing was rudely awakened by a massive tremor which shook the foundation of the home he occupied on Sacramento Street (adjacent to the east side of the present location of Nam Kue Chinese School). Feeling the earthquake shake the house, he tumbled out of bed, pulled on his clothing and ran outside. He was stunned by

what he saw. Some of the shanty-like building had been reduced to rubble, and in the distance, he could make out the shadows of fallen buildings.

Thinking quickly, he grabbed two suitcases that he could carry and went around the house filling them up with personal papers, jewelry and keepsake items, with cash in one and clothing in the other. He was worried about the con-

dition of his new cannery in Oakland, so he made his way through the crowds toward the ferry dock. According to later historical reports, Chinatown was destroyed:

> "The earthquake had lasted for forty-eight seconds. The streets tore open, debris crashing onto the sidewalks. Water burst from split mains, people hurled flailing into the air. City Hall, a monolith of steel and concrete, crumbled instantly, leaving only its framework standing. Chinatown, as with the rest of the city, found itself reduced to a state of utter dysfunction.... The tenements had been poorly

> constructed and rickety, and now many fell, their residents escaping into the streets…With many water mains broken, the fire department had only a limited supply of water. As a last resort, they began using dynamite in an attempt to create firebreaks…
>
> This strategy had some unfortunate results. The west end of Chinatown caught fire when a group of firefighters, having run out of dynamite, resorted to black powder to clear buildings along Kearney Street; the blasts were too weak to vaporize the structures, but strong enough to rocket flaming wood onto structures at Chinatown's edge, setting them on fire.
>
> Overturned stoves and candles, meanwhile, kindled other parts of the neighborhood. The major streets soon became furnaces, and Chinatown was doomed. Thousands of residents abandoned attempts to retrieve their possessions in the rubble and ran screaming from the fire storm. Some made it down Market Street to the Ferry Building; others made their way to open spaces such as Washington Square."[28]

A KINSMAN TO THE RESCUE

As in San Francisco, the whites in Oakland harbored latent racist sentiments:

> "One of the evils springing from the late disaster to San Francisco, one that menaces Oakland exceedingly, but that seems to have escaped attention, is

---

[28] Nick Kolakowshi, *Earth Dragon Trembled: San Francisco's Chinatown and the Great Earthquake of 1906*, medium.com, February 6, 2018.

> the great influx of Chinese into this city from San Francisco. Not only have they pushed outward the limits of Oakland's heretofore constructed and insignificant Chinatown, but they have settled themselves in large colonies throughout residence parts of the city, bringing with them their vices and their filth....
>
> "It has been found necessary to put up the sign, 'No Chinese or Japanese wanted here.' White families in the neighborhood are moving away, unwilling to be surrounded by the degradation, the filth and the vice that a Chinatown means."[29]

The story of the plight of the Chinese refugees at the hands of the whites was never covered by the white newspapers in the West. Not until the centennial of the "Great San Francisco Earthquake of April 1906" was the public made aware of the heroics of Lew Hing in a *Wall Street Journal* article dated April 8, 2006, and through a Chinese Historical Society of America booklet which contained the following story from *Sing Tao Daily* on April 15, 2006:

Lew Hing: A Kinsman to the Rescue

By Connie Young Yu

Lew Hing: A Kinsman To The Rescue

by Connie Young Yu

"Oakland was not prepared for the sudden influx of refugees, and the Chinese who escaped there by ferry received the worst situation, kept in an

---

[29] The Oakland Herald, April 27, 1906 page 1c5

open area at Lake Merritt, with meager provisions and without shelter from the soaking rains that were to come. At this dire moment, one San Francisco Chinese, Lew Hing, took the initiative and launched his own relief effort in Oakland.

"He was an established man of means, but on April 18, like everyone in the devastated city, Lew Hing had lost his home and business. Fortunately, his family was on a visit to China and no one was injured in the cannery building that the Lews called home. Although he was unable to save any of his belongings in the rubble, Lew Hing had purpose and a destination as he waited among the desperate throngs of his fellow countrymen for the Ferry to Oakland…

"…With the success of his first, he started another cannery in 1904, the Pacific Coast Canning Company in Oakland, a most propitious choice of location, at 12th and Pine Street.

"It was the cannery he established in the quiet town of Oakland that would play such a major role in the recovery of the Chinese community…

"…Once in Oakland Lew Hing rose to meet the needs of his people. His Pacific Coast Canning Company employed Italian and Portuguese immigrants as well as Chinese. It was a large property on two blocks. Lew Hing directed his workers to set temporary housing and distribute emergency provisions. Soon the cannery grounds would be a field of tents with capable cooks making hot Cantonese meals for the hungry refugees. At last, the exhausted Chinese were part of a familiar community, safe and protected until they could be on their feet again. (Chinese Historical Society of America)

"In the meantime, the Chinese in other cities mobilized and in a subtle response to the treatment of the Chinese in San Francisco, the following was reported.

"When news of the catastrophe spread around the world, numerous contributions for relief immediately began flowing in. The Chinese Imperial Government remitted 40,000 taels, equivalent to U.S. $30,668. The governor general Cen Chunxuan of Guangdong initiated a drive for donations and appropriated 60,000 taels from the government treasury, equivalent to U.S. $40,000. The governor general of Hubei, Zhang Zhidong, donated 20,000 taels. Chinese living as far away as Peru, Singapore, and cities of Yokohama and Osaka in Japan all contributed relief funds. The total reached U.S. $229,994.54. Later, part of the remainder of the relief funds was used to finance the rebuilding of Chinatown."[30]

The Associated Press, from the Texas *Dallas News*, April 24, 1906, printed this article:

CHINESE RAISING FUND.

Will Contribute to Relief of All Suffers Alike.

"New York, April 24. — The Chinese Merchants' Association met last night and discussed the best

[30] Him Mark Lai, *Becoming Chinese American: A History of Communities and Institutions*, 2004, AltaMira Press. p 94-95

means of affording aid to the San Francisco sufferers, especially the Chinese. Shah Kaifu, the Chinese Consul, was present and read this telegram, received on Sunday night, from Consul Chung Pao Hsi of San Francisco:

"Chinatown is entirely destroyed and our people are in great distress. Send whatever money you can collect for our people to Chin Fook & Co., 373 Ninth Street, Oakland. CHUNG PAO HSI."

Segregated Chinese Camp after 1906 Earthquake

"In addition to the $2,700 handed over to the New York City Mayor's relief fund committee, the Chinese expect to raise at least $3,000.

"It was grand of President Roosevelt to take upon himself to see that everyone shared alike in the relief," said Consul Shah. "It is only another proof that he is a friend of all mankind. We can not

> be less generous with our contributions than he with his wise counsels. I believe that whatever aid the Chinese of New York should give should be divided up among all sufferers. It is wise to turn the contribution already raised over to New York Mayor McClellan and the committee can not do better with what they get in the future."
>
> "The question of the disposition of the future funds was not decided, but it is likely that the committee will follow the advice of consul. The Chinese have made it plain that the aid from them is not to be confined to members of their own race."

Lew Hing's timing on building and opening the cannery was pure luck. It was fully operational and would continue through the earthquake. For Lew Hing, there was a silver lining in the destruction of Chinatown—the racism of the whites presented him with the opportunity to cast himself as a major philanthropist among the Chinese.

THE WHITE DEVIL'S LIES

There was a specific reference to the Chinese in San Francisco after the earthquake in the official report by the Army to Secretary of War Taft. This followed General Funston's orders that the Chinese *not be served* immediately after the earthquake, prompting complaints by the Empress of China through the Chinese Legation in Washington D.C. to President Roosevelt, who ordered Acting Secretary Oliver to send a telegram to General Funston that all refugees were to be treated alike a week after the earthquake. Here is part of that report.

Earthquake in California, April 18, 1906.
Special Report of
Maj. Adolphus W Greely,
U.S.A. Commanding the Pacific Division.

Sir: In accordance with the instructions of the Hon. William H. Taft, Secretary of War, under date of June 29, 1906, I have the honor to submit herewith a comprehensive report of the services of the United States Army in connection with the recent earthquake and conflagration in the city of San Francisco, Cal. and the relief measures rendered necessary by these disasters….

The report of operations of Brigadier-General Funston, who was temporarily in command during my absence, from April 18 to 22, follows in full:

RELIEF FOR THE CHINESE

It is gratifying to report that neither in San Francisco has any relief committee shown discrimination against the Chinese, and this line of action of the civilian organization has been consistently followed by the army. Far greater number of the Chinese left San Francisco, and while many are scattered through adjacent towns, they have largely returned to work.

It was the consensus of opinion that the Chinese could be best cared for in separate camps; this policy was followed in San Francisco and Oakland. An excellently arranged camp was constructed at Fort Winfield Scott on the Presidio grounds, the only objection thereto being the distance from the inhabited parts of the city, but as practically none of the Chinese are day laborers, no special hardship has resulted therefrom. The food is good, the bedding is neat, and the sanitary conditions excellent. This camp has dwindled to 50 occupants, and is kept up at army expense, pending final arrangement with the Chinese consul for its transfer elsewhere.

The Chinese minister to the United States visited both this camp and the Oakland camp. He later expressed to me his satisfaction at the comfortable manner in which his destitute countrymen have been treated. The agent of the Six Companies stated that many of them were living better than ever before. Their comfortable condition is known to me both by personal inspection and by daily reports.

The Chinese camp in Oakland was probably the best camp in that city; sanitation, food, and shelter being excellent. The first secretary of the Chinese legation and the Chinese consul expressed their satisfaction and admiration for the comfort of the camp and the prevailing system. Later, as mentioned under Oakland relief operations, the care of the Chinese was assumed by the Chinese Minister."

This is an excerpt from the Oakland and Alameda section of the same report:

OAKLAND AND ALAMEDA

The Chinese, in a camp established independently on Lake Merritt, were cared for in the same systematic and satisfactory manner as were the occupants at Adams Point. Under a Chinese superintendent, the camp was maintained in excellent condition, its occupants never causing trouble, and although located in the resident portion of the city, it was so admirably handled that its presence was never a

> cause of complaint. His excellency the Chinese Minister inspected carefully the Chinese camp near the end of May, and was so gratified with the proper care of his destitute countrymen that he arranged for the future location, under Major Erwin's supervision, of the destitute Chinese in permanent wooden structures."

What undoubtedly prompted this sanitized report was the following telegram from McGee, secretary to the Chief of Staff, to President Roosevelt with a copy to General Funston:

> General Funston April 23. 1906
> San Francisco.
>
> Following message has been sent today:
>
> Dr. Edward T. Devine,
> Red Cross, San Francisco
>
> According to newspaper reports, suffering and destitution liable to become particularly great among Chinese. Nothing known of the matter here beyond press reports. At suggestion of President, I am authorized to say in name of Secretary Taft, president of society that Red Cross work should be done wholly without regard to persons and just as much for Chinese as any others. Please see that this is done. Secretary of War will instruct General Funston to cooperate with you in this matter. Have already given to First Secretary of Chinese Legation, who has left for San Francisco, a letter to you asking that he be extended all

possible assistance in relieving distress of Chinese.

McGee
Secretary

President directs you furnish same shelter and camping facilities to Chinese as to others and that you cooperate with Red Cross in relieving suffering or destitution among them. Use your own discretion as to whether special camps shall be established for them. Government supplies must be furnished and Government protection afforded to all alike and all suffering relieved without regard to nationality.

Oliver
Acting Secretary of War

This telegram calling the local officials to task elicited the usual denials by telegrams dated April 24, 1906:

Telegram from Major General Greely:

"To the Military Secretary, ...Nothing could be more contrary to the truth..."

And signers of this telegram included the leading anti-Chinese racist, James D. Phelan:

"To President Theodore Roosevelt....All reports that the people of the administration, or the relief committee of San Francisco are making any distinction between relieving, succoring or protecting the Chinese, and any other people differing in color or race, are totally false and unfounded...."

And from the *San Francisco Chronicle*, Editorial Page, April 26, 1906, there was pushback, and an interesting reference to the "restoration" of Chinatown:

> "It is believed in this city that reports were sent East to the effect that the Chinese were being neglected in the work of relief. If so, never was there fouler slander of an unfortunate community...but measures are already in progress to restore it [Chinatown] in another and better location, but where it will not be showplace in the middle of the city...."

CITY FATHERS SAY NO TO CHINATOWN 1906

The earthquake gave a rare respite to the years of enmity between the Sam Yup and Sze Yup merchants; they both now had a common enemy, the city leaders.

San Francisco city leaders had no intentions of letting Chinatown rebuild. Chinatown occupied some of the most valuable real estate in San Francisco, with its twelve-square -blocks set between Nob Hill and the financial center of the West. Echoing their sentiment, *The Overland Monthly* stated that the fire had "reclaimed for civilization and cleanliness the Chinatown ghetto and no Chinatown will be permitted in the borders of the city."

Mayor Eugene Schmitz had been elected with the support of the very labor forces that had been antagonizing the Chinese community for decades, and he had no intention of disappointing his constituents by allowing things to revert to the way they were. He thought, along with many other prominent political and economic figures, that the Chinese community should be moved to the outskirts of the city.

Eight days after the disaster, on April 26, a General Relief Committee proposal to gather all Chinese into the temporary camp at the Presidio was quickly adopted and a committee comprised of Abraham "Abe" Ruef, James D. Phelan, Jeremiah Deneen, Dr. James W. Ward, president of the Health Commission, and Methodist minister Dr. Thomas Fiben, chairman, was formed to take charge of the question of the permanent location of the Chinese quarter.

From a strictly political standpoint, this was a remarkable committee because Abe Ruef and James D. Phelan were arch-enemies. Ex-Mayor Phelan had helped spark the graft investigation which would ultimately lead to Ruef serving time at San Quentin State Prison. Ruef was the undisputed "boss" of California, and served as the Southern Pacific Railway's political point man in San Francisco. Their common ground was abiding racism and hatred for the Chinese, and despite the total devastation of San Francisco, relocation of Chinatown was a major priority.

Hunter's Point as the location to relocate the Chinese was not a new idea; industrialist John Partridge had previously proposed an "Oriental City" at Hunters Point and at that time, Mayor Schmitz supported it.

Hunter's Point sat on an expanse of mud flats. At the time of the earthquake, it was an area of slaughterhouses. One can only imagine the stench in the air, or the large amounts of animal waste polluting the environment. For the city's political establishment, the idea of moving Chinatown to Hunter's Point was so favorable that it arose again and again in discussion, even as other locations were considered and discarded.

The Committee on the Location of Chinatown began, with the help of General Funston, to bring together in one place the few Chinese left in San Francisco, in preparation for moving them to Hunter's Point.

With virtually all of Chinatown destroyed, most of its inhabitants had fled to Oakland, other cities in the East Bay, or were huddled in the refugee camp at the west end of the Presidio. Those who tried to return to Chinatown found it guarded by soldiers with orders to shoot to kill Chinese, while white looters were allowed with wagons to roam through the ruins looting the residences and stores.

In a poorly planned evacuation, Chinese refugees were shuttled to various relief camps all over the city. A temporary camp on Van Ness prompted relocation to the Presidio because Phelan argued that the site would prove difficult to dismantle once the Chinese settled again in a location so close to the original Chinatown.

There were 500 refugees in that encampment as of April 26. City fathers then considered an area next to the Presidio Golf Links. However, "Charles S. Wheeler, who led a delegation of residents and property owners, called upon the military authorities at the Presidio and objected to the establishment of the Oriental quarters so close to their homes, where the summer zephyrs would blow the odors of Chinatown into their front doors."[31]

One of the most prominent protesters and a member of Mayor Schmitz's Committee of Fifty, was Benjamin Ide Wheeler, then-president of the University of California (1899-1919). Ironically, he professed an academic interest in things Oriental and was a member of the American Oriental Society. Perhaps, however, his true colors were revealed

[31] *San Francisco Chronicle*, April 28, 1906.

during World War I—his widely-known German sympathies and admiration for the Kaiser eventually brought suspicion upon him, prompting his retirement as President of the University of California after the Armistice in 1919.

Heeding these protests, the army summarily moved the Chinese to Fort Point on April 27. In the end, *The San Francisco Relief Survey,* compiling various aspects of the city's recovery, found that: "…a population of 10,000 Chinese was represented by only 20 families drawing rations." Furthermore, the Relief Survey claimed, "[the Chinese] did not ask for much….not over 140 applications for rehabilitation were assigned to Chinese; ten thousand dollars is a liberal estimate for the value of relief given to the [Chinese]."

The presence of Chinatown in the center of the city always rankled the whites and as early as 1880, they had wanted to get rid of Chinatown. At that time, it was ostensibly the conditions in Chinatown that drew such widespread criticism as to cause the Board of Health, responding to political pressure, to issue a resolution formally condemning Chinatown as a "nuisance."

"The Chinese cancer must be cut out of the heart of our city, root and branch, if we have any regard for its future sanitary welfare…with all the vacant and health territory around the city, it is a shame that the very centre be surrendered and abandoned to this health-defying and law-defying population. We, therefore, recommend that the portion of the city here described be condemned as a nuisance; and we call upon proper authorities to take necessary steps for its abatement without delay.[32]

But the Chinese fought back.

---

[32] Workingmen's Party of California, Anti-Chinese Council, "Chinatown Declared a Nuisance!" (San Francisco, 1880), p.6.

"The Chinatown community was less than thrilled at the prospect, but for April and May generally remained silent on the issue. Many found themselves too busy trying to repair their lives: newspapers reported that Chinese property owners intended to begin anew where their holdings had been, and that 'Chinese leaders had contacted famous lawyers who….said that anyone who owned or leased properties could legally build new buildings.'"[33]

For the city's leaders, however, a sticking point developed that had nothing to do with building ownership. If the Chinese merchants were forced to move, it would disrupt both tax revenues and duties from trade with China. In 1905, Chinese merchants were thought to have paid almost fifteen million dollars in import duties; if they left the city altogether, or even paused their operations, it would have resulted in significant financial losses for San Francisco.

Leung Seng, 1906, Minister of the Chinese Legation

This point was made abundantly clear by representatives of the government of China. Leung Seng, Minister of the Chinese Legation in Washington, arrived in Oakland within a few days of the earthquake and met with Chung Pao Hsi, China's Consul General in San Francisco. They in turn met with Governor Pardee in Oakland, and told him of the Empress-Dowager's displeasure with the plan, and that the

[33] Nick Kolakowski, *Earth Dragon Trembled: San Francisco's Chinatown and the Great Earthquake of 1906*, medium.com, February 6, 2018

government of China would rebuild its San Francisco Consulate in the heart of Old Chinatown.

Coupled with this stiff resistance was the threat to move the shipping to Los Angeles, resulting in lost profits, jobs and taxes. The relocation plan died a swift death.

DIRECT FAMILY CONTROL OF UNDERGROUND ACTIVITIES

1906

With Chinatown in ruins, all illegal activities and the money it brought in came to a halt. Lew Hing's chief concern was how to keep the spigot for cash flowing for his ventures. That would require Chinatown to be rebuilt and repopulated as quickly as possible. While he tended to his new venture in Oakland, his old friend Lew Yu approached him.

Lew Yu, Lew Hing's first friend in America and business partner in Hing Kee & Co., had overseen the public welfare fund for Loong Kong from its inception. In America since 1869 and now nearing his mid fifties, he was ready to return to his family. He appealed to his friend and partner in business:

"Lew Hing, your future and family is rooted here now but my family is rooted in China. The shaking of the earth and destruction of Chinatown tells me it is time to be with my family. Please find someone else to handle Mu Tin."

Lew Hing was unstinting in his affection and praise for his friend:

"My old friend, we have been together through good times and not so good times from when your wise counsel helped me when my elder brother perished and left me with Hing Kee. The gods have smiled on me for having such a good and loyal friend. Instead of traveling back and forth all these years to see your family, I agree it is time for you to be

with them all the time. Please accept this gift of cash to ease your retirement and provide for your children and grand-children for their future."

Before Lew Yu departed, in September 1906, Lew Hing summoned Quan Yeen from China to take over leadership of Mu Tin. Upon Quan Yeen's arrival, Lew Hing met him at the dock and after both surveyed the destruction of what once was Chinatown, they took the ferry to Oakland. Similar to San Francisco, the new Oakland Chinatown was segregated from the rest of the city. Already it was overcrowded with refugees, makeshift businesses and hastily set-up offices for the Chinese consulate, Six Companies and other social organizations.

"I have purchased this house at 272 Eighth Street for you and Yuet-yung and your children. My family lives directly across the street at 271-273." Lew Hing said.

After settling in, Quan Yeen accompanied Lew Hing around the new cannery where they met Lew Yu. Back in the office after showing him the vault, they sat down to discuss business.

"My old friend, Lew Yu, is retiring to China to spend his last years in the glory of his family. I need you to assume the responsibility of overseeing the activities of Mu Tin. You will personally count the money from each night and keep the books. You will adjust the count so your family and mine will have ample funds to live on as well as funds I will use to invest. Be sure that the books show there is sufficient reserves for public relations purposes. Also, to keep above suspicion, never get your hands dirty, use only Loong Kong lieutenants you trust to hire professionals to handle the street-level tasks."

Relying on Quan Yeen and the Mu Tin associates to keep the spigot in Chinatown open was a forbidding challenge for Quan Yeen. As a dutiful son-in-law, he accepted the assignment and purchased a .32 and four magazines of ammunition for protection. With fellow clansmen, he practiced shooting. In time, he felt comfortable and confident enough to use it.

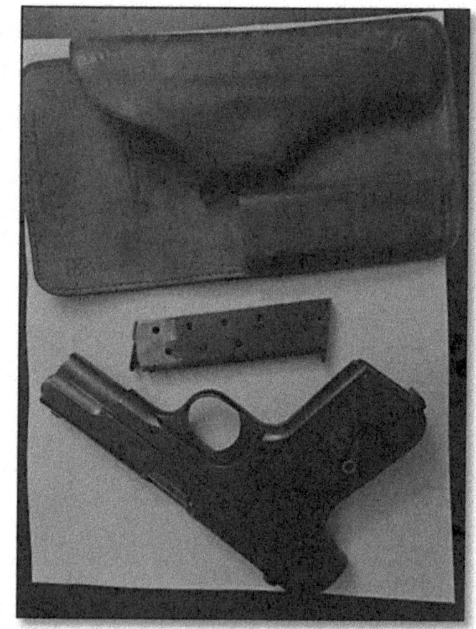

Quan Yeen's gun and holster

Quan Yeen knew this change in direction would not allow him to return to Fresno where he and his family had business interests. He traveled to Fresno to sell the dry goods store and liquidate other interests.

In time, Quan Yeen grew into the role of head of Mu Tin. But he had yet to be tested. That came nearly a year after, in 1908, when remnants of the Tongs, attempting to reassert themselves, chose to rob a Mu Tin gambling house.

Four erstwhile Tong individuals burst into the basement of a Loong Kong-controlled gambling house. They were *Bow Hao Doi* (hatchet men/thugs) with their queues tied up on top of their heads covered by hats, and masks covering their faces. They had caught the guards by surprise at the door and pushing them in at gunpoint, entered the gambling den. In Sze Yup dialect, a gunman carrying a shotgun shouted to everyone to face the walls and not to move.

One of the gunmen then went to the tables and began scooping up the cash. Two others went along the walls, holding guns to the backs of the customers and ordered them to empty out their pockets of cash, remove the mostly jade jewelry, pocket watches with jade watch fobs, jade stick pins and other gold jewelry.

As swiftly as they entered, they fled into the night. One of the guards at the door ran immediately to Quan Yeen's residence to report the robbery. Hurriedly dressing, he summoned his bodyguard and accompanied the guard back to the gambling den.

Having read American detective novels while in Fresno, Quan Yeen recalled the investigative techniques illustrated in those books. He first had all of the customers give him their names and where they could be found, promising to keep each name confidential by assigning each a number. Then he instructed each to make a list of cash and jewelry and other valuables they claimed to have lost. When finished, he dismissed them with the assurance that he would find the robbers and recover their valuables. Next, he questioned all the guards. He was reasonably certain they knew nothing of the plan to rob the gambling den. Satisfied he had done all he could at that time, he returned to his residence to plan a strategy for locating the thieves.

Word of the robbery leaked out into the community the next day and, unlike the normal response by a gambling house robbed by thieves—shrugging off the losses and doubling the guards—Quan Yeen wanted to send a message to the Tongs to deter further robberies. As with other robberies, a reward was offered but generally the residents were too afraid of retaliation if they spoke up.

The next day, the Mu Tin men began circulating through Chinatown, listening to the gossiping in the stores, markets, family associations and other places.

In one store, as one of the men was chatting with another shopper, he noticed a young man, ill-dressed but wearing an expensive jade ring, purchasing goods with a large bill. As he left, he followed a safe distance away until he watched him enter a building on Washington Street. Hurrying back to Quan Yeen, he reported his discovery.

Quan Yeen and a fellow clansman quickly went to that address and staked out the entrance. The clansman stood in the shadows until nightfall waiting for the thief to emerge. As he emerged, the clansman accosted him and with a gun at his back, brought him back to the gambling den where Quan Yeen waited. There, the guards identified the pants and shirt on the man as clothes worn by the thief the night before, and with the addition of the ring and a roll of large bills, were certain he was one of the robbers.

They interrogated him to reveal the names and locations of the other three thieves. Initially, he refused to talk but breaking several of his fingers forced the names from his mouth. They kept him tied up in the back room behind the gambling den.

Quan Yeen had to act quickly as once it was known that this man was missing, the other three thieves were likely to flee. They learned that the second thief also lived in the same building as the first one, and he was soon easily captured and brought to the gambling den as well. Fearful for his life, he told Quan Yeen everything he knew, including that the ring-leader was planning to leave on the next ship for China and the last thief was going by train to Sacramento to hide out there.

The first lesson Quan Yeen had learned from the American detective novels was to cover possible exits from town. He had clansmen stake out both the shipping office and the train station. The next morning, they stopped the ring leader as he emerged from the steamship office and, with two pistols from under their jackets, escorted him to Loong Kong. Similarly, as the last thief sat in the train station waiting for the train, two men sat on either side of him with guns showing and marched him back to Chinatown.

In the rough and tumble Chinese underworld, Quan Yeen needed to send a message that Mu Tin, under new leadership, was not to be trifled with. That night, the first thief "jumped" from a building in Chinatown. The next day, white fisherman discovered a "Chinaman" floating in the harbor, his throat slit. That next afternoon, hikers found another "Chinaman" shot in the head. The ringleader was found in the middle of Dupont Gai, hands bound behind his back, throat slit and eyes gouged out and a large bill wadded up and shoved in his mouth. Quan Yeen cleaned his gun, replacing a bullet missing from the magazine.

The customers were thrilled when their valuables and some cash were returned to them. Business at the gambling house increased and, as word of the safety of the premises spread, more Mu Tin gambling houses along with opium dens appeared. Despite occasional robberies of gambling dens, none of those operated by Mu Tin were hit. Quan Yeen, however, did have occasion to use his gun at other times to remind those who would interfere or had insulted a Loong Kong member or his family.

"CHINATOWN, MY CHINATOWN"

1908

Tin Pan Alley songwriters Jean Schwartz and William Jerome wrote what was considered their most successful song, "Chinatown, My Chinatown," in the same year San Francisco Chinatown was destroyed by The Great Earthquake of 1906. For a brief time, the image of the Chinese as interlopers was countered by a rebuilt Chinatown more to the liking of the whites.

White property owners who comprised 80 percent ownership of lots in Chinatown had resisted pressure to consider the interests of the City at large. In May of 1906, they immediately signed new lease agreements with the Chinese. Their opposition to relocation was purely financial, not because they were friends of or sympathetic to the Chinese. The white landlords remained supportive because the Chinese paid high rents, were reliable tenants and never complained.

The renewal of leases effectively defeated the relocation effort, and Chinese merchants organized to play a major role in the planning for a new Chinatown. For the remainder of 1906 and 1907, merchants held many meetings.

Before the earthquake, Lew Hing was the major investor in an investor group which established the Sing Chong import/export store. Located at the entrance to Chinatown on the corner of California and Dupont Streets, it was the business "vehicle" for Lew clansmen and other selected countrymen to qualify under the exception to the 1882 Chinese Exclusion Act as Merchants. This most sought-after status allowed the "merchant" to travel back and forth to secure money and goods for their businesses or other reasons. The scheme had assisted Lew Hing in securing loyal allies in Chinatown among a broad cross-section of influential figures in the community.

The general manager of the store was Look Tin Eli, fluent in English and Chinese. Raised in Mendocino, where he attended a local school before his father shipped him to China for further education, he was familiar with dealings with whites.

Re-built Sing Chong building at of California and Dupont (renamed Grant Avenue)

When the earthquake destroyed the building housing Sing Chong, Lew Hing immediately entered into a lease with the property owner and gave Look the assignment of rebuilding the business with the following instruction: *"The Owners of Sing Fat — the store on Dupont Street directly across the street that was destroyed by fire — is being rebuilt as a tourist-like oriental style building to attract the attention of the rich tourists who will ride the California Street Cable Car line. We should do the same for Sing Chong."*

Look Tin Eli successfully completed his assignment and then, at Lew Hing's direction, he convinced other property owners that building a tourist friendly Dupont Street would increase the rents they could charge. In his own words, Look waxed poetic in a newspaper article about the new Sing Chong Bazaar, but he also took sole credit for making Chinatown a tourist attraction.

Our New Oriental City —
Veritable Fairy Palaces Filled with the Choicest Treasures of the Orient

By Look Tin Eli

San Francisco enjoys the unique distinction of being the one spot in the Occidental world where the traveler may feast his senses on all the treasures of the Orient with none of the hardships and worries incidental to travel in a fierce tropical climate, not to mention the most primitive facilities for transportation.

San Francisco's new Chinatown is so much more beautiful, which the united press of San Francisco declared could never be resuscitated. And every American citizen realizes how much these quiet, industrious people have done for the commerce of Greater San Francisco.

The new Chinatown—Beautiful is simply a revelation to the Eastern tourist who has the least modicum of artistic taste or appreciation of things beautiful. Let him take his stand, say at the corner of Dupont and California, and take in the fascinating vista down the former street as far as Pacific; he will enjoy a view which for fantastic Oriental architecture and color scheme cannot be duplicated in the wide world, not even in the Orient, for the reason that in that interesting country, the contrasts are entirely too pronounced, and a magnificent palace

> is frequently surrounded by dozens of ordinary shacks and mat sheds. Let him take his first view any bright, sunny day, then let him return at dark and witness the wonderful transformation when the hundreds of thousands of electric lights bathe the streets and facades of the wildly fantastic buildings in a blaze of glory as bright as midday.
>
> Greater San Francisco may well be proud of its new Chinatown and well may she write it down as one of her most valued assets, for it is the one distinguishing mark which proclaims her different from any other great city in the whole civilized world. And the Chinese residents of the city are certainly deserving of the unstinted praise for the pluck and courage they have shown in the rehabilitation of their particular quarter, artistic, and so much more emphatically Oriental than the old Chinatown, the destruction of which great writers and artists have wept over for two years, [and which] is not worthy to be mentioned in the same breath."[34]

Compared to the usual anti-Chinese slant of the news media in San Francisco, the opening of the newly completed Sing Chong Bazaar brought praise from the whites.

Gateway to the Orient of the Golden Gate

> Truly the gateway to the Orient of the Golden Gate is the Sing Chong bazaar at California and Dupont Streets. San Francisco's Chinatown, known the world over, holds no [other] mart where tapestries and silks from the remotest corners of Asia, ebony

---

[34] Western Press Association, *San Francisco: The Metropolis of the West*, 1917, p. 90-93

and ivory carvings, teak wood furniture and hammered brass vases from the Far East vie in greater splendor and variety.

This bazaar is one of the sights of San Francisco. To the tourist from the East, it is an introduction and invitation to Chinatown. To the curiosity seeker from the city or elsewhere it is a revelation and delight. Situated at the beginning of Dupont Street, the main thoroughfare of the Oriental quarter, it is always the first place visited. By reason of its unique showing and distinctiveness, it usually is the last remembered.

Five stories high, surmounted by a typical Chinese tower, which at night is illuminated with studdings of electric lights, commodious in its interior as any American department store, the Sing Chong Bazaar is a startling but pleasing combination of flamboyant, Far East gaudiness of color and clear-cut Yankee enterprise and up-to-dateness. Chinese clerks, speaking precise English, attend customers with Oriental politeness.

In all important trading centers of Japan and China are posted expert buyers for this bazaar. The Sing Chong company has a factory of its own in Canton.

The Sing Chong Bazaar is a success because it is well managed. The president of the company is a multimillionaire importing- and exporting-merchant prince of Canton, China. The direct management in San Francisco is in the hands of the importer's son, Loo Chuck Wan, and Look Tin Eli,

> a prominent native Californian who has a wide record of business success. He is a director in the Canton Bank and formerly was a wholesale grocer.
>
> The variety of goods to be had at the bazaar is large, a stock of $200,000 being carried. Among many others these are the principal lines of goods handled: bronzes, porcelains, silk embroideries, kimonos, cloisonné, satsumas, handkerchiefs, shawls, gowns, beads, bedspreads and silken underwear.[35]

Then, the Western Press Association published an article on Chinatown, possibly after interviewing Look Tin Eli:

> ...For the edification of our readers, here is a brief history of the rehabilitation of San Francisco's Chinatown, and how it came about that the idea of Oriental architecture and coloring was suggested and carried out.
>
> To the intelligent observer the question naturally suggests itself: Who is responsible for this wonderful accomplishment? The thing never occurred by mere accident, nor could it possibly have been thrown together from the ideas of hundreds of builders. For there is evidence that the scheme of architecture and color must have originated in some mastermind; that some individual must have created the model that others might follow his example, thus completing the scheme as we see it today.
>
> Immediately after the destruction of the city by the great fire of April 1906, Look Tin Eli, who had been general manager of the original Sing Chong Bazaar at the corner of Dupont and California

[35] *San Francisco Call*, Sunday, April 26, 1908, p. 67.

Streets, where the magnificent new bazaar now stands, began laying plans for the erection of a new structure on lines far more ambitious than had ever before been dreamed of by the Chinese residents of the old days. Look Tin Eli knew what he wanted, but he also realized that the project was far too heavy for one man to ever attempt; he realized that an immense amount of capital would be necessary to successfully accomplish his dream. He also knew very well where the capital might be found.

He knew of the untold billions of hidden wealth that lay rusting in the secret vaults of the merchant princes in China, and he determined to submit his plans and ideas to a certain millionaire of his acquaintance of Hong Kong and Canton, Loo Koon Tong, and his son, Loo Chuck Wan. As soon as the project was fully explained to these two gentlemen, they immediately informed Look Tin Eli that his proposition was accepted, and that they stood ready to furnish all the capital necessary to the "extent of three million dollars." His one stipulation was that his son, Loo Chuck Wan, was to be made associate manager of the firm and that the whole scheme be incorporated under the laws of the State of California. This was consummated as soon as the plans of the architect were drawn in the rough.

Here was the chance for Look Tin Eli to carry out his plan of an ideal Oriental city, for he was confident that once he had set the pace, others must follow suit. The results speak for itself, and those of our own people who have a love for the beautiful may thank Loo Koon Tong, Loo Chuck Wan and

> Look Tin Eli of the Sing Chong Bazaar for their Chinatown Beautiful.
>
> The Sing Chong Bazaar, on the corner of Dupont and California Streets, stands today as the most magnificent treasure house for Oriental goods and works of art in the world. The concern is capitalized for two hundred thousand dollars, and carries a stock valued at full three hundred and fifty thousand, with additional goods ordered that will cost over half a million American dollars. What other association of three men can boast of having done more for the commerce of Greater San Francisco?
>
> Elsewhere in Chinatown are other splendid Oriental bazaars and business houses. At any hour of the day or evening, admiring tourists, travelers and spectators, and buyers in general may be seen before their beautiful show-windows, and inspecting the rich, rare and original curios, silks and other art treasures of China and Japan.[36]

In 1906 when the Sze Yup and Sam Yup merchants guilds formed the Chinese Chamber of Commerce, Lew Hing promoted Look Tin Eli as Secretary of the organization, pointing out his successful job at Sing Chong Bazaar. With this appointment, Look could continue the master plan Lew Hing had for Dupont Street.

To help create more businesses to fill the stores on Dupont Street, Lew Hing used the "merchant" scheme to personally finance Nanjing Fook Wah, another import/export store at the corner of Grant Avenue and Sacramento

[36] Western Press Association, *San Francisco: Metropolis of the West*, 1917, p. 90-93.

Street, one block from Sing Chong Bazaar. Simultaneous with the opening of that store, he also led an investor group to finance the new upscale Republic Hotel conveniently located directly across the street from Nanjing Fook Wah.

ESTABLISHING THE CANTON BANK 1908

However, Lew Hing's plan for consolidating his power in Chinatown was not finished. He had been long thinking of how to start a bank for Chinatown, but he had no experience. The earthquake had provided an answer. Look Poon Shan, Look Tin Eli's brother, and Isaac P. Allen had been bank executives at the Russo-Asiatic Bank and lost their jobs when it became a correspondent bank after the earthquake destroyed its location. Lew Hing suggested to Look Tin Eli

Inside the Canton Bank

that if there was a bank from which merchants could borrow money to reestablish their businesses, it would speed up the redevelopment of Chinatown. He further offered that he would be willing to invest in the bank if Look's brother and Allen would run it. Look met with his brother and Allen.

"Many of the other communities have their own banks such as the Italians and Irish, the Chinese should have one as well. Would you and Allen be interested in helping run a bank for the Chinese?" asked Look Tin Eli.

Look Poon Shan responded, "To open a bank, the minimum capital must be $300,000. If you can collect the minimum capital, Allen and I will guide you through the process of opening a bank."

Look Tin Eli went back to Lew Hing with the news to which Lew Hing advised how to successfully gather investors: *"As secretary of the Chinese Chamber of Commerce, set up a time for me to make a presentation to the members on the potential of our community having its own bank."*

Lew Hing made a presentation to the members extolling the benefits of a Chinese bank to make loans to Chinese businesses, provide a secure place for residents to keep their cash, and enhance the reputation of the Chinese community. After his presentation, he asked the Chamber to pass a resolution approving the forming of a bank if the initial capital of $300,000 could be raised.

Lew Hing then stated, "I will invest $10,000 of the necessary capital." The bank was granted a license in 1907 and opened in 1908 at the corner of Kearney and Clay Streets with Look Poon Shan as General Manager and Isaac Allen as Assistant General Manager. Lew Hing was a member of the original board of directors.

CHINATOWN RE-OPENS

1908 - 1910

In 1908, Grant Avenue reopened to great fanfare as a stylish tourist attraction for whites, distracting their attention from the rebuilding of the rest of Chinatown where gambling houses, opium dens and brothels would open.

Lew Hing's stature in the Chinese community continued to ascend due to his philanthropic gestures and prominent influence in the rebuilding of Chinatown. Loong Kong was still the largest and most powerful family association in Chinatown and had expanded its influence throughout the cities and towns in America. Lew Hing was a major financial contributor to the cost of rebuilding the Association meeting hall destroyed by the earthquake. With this donation, Lew Hing was assured to be part of the leadership going forward and Quan Yeen the head of Mu Tin.

Loong Kong, as a "family" association, unlike the secretive Tongs, was viewed differently by the white authorities. They were considered peaceful, and their activities beneficial in that they kept the clansmen preoccupied with recreational releases such as gambling and opium smoking, along with the opera. All these activities were controlled by the Mu Tin, and money continued to flow into the vaults at Pacific Coast Canning.

SIX

TRUSTED LIEUTENANTS

DAUGHTER YUET-YUNG AND SON-IN-LAW QUAN YEEN

As Lew Hing's focus and attention turned to interacting with the white world, Quan Yeen and Yuet-yung became his backstops in the Chinese community.

Lew Hing's oldest child, his daughter Yuet-yung, was what he wished his son Lew Gin-gow would have been. If that had been the case, his empire might have survived the various challenges it faced.

From an early age, Yuet-yung was a stubborn child, having more of her qualities of her father than her mother. She was headstrong and reveled in being hard-nosed and rebellious. This attitude was fostered by her early environment of constantly being in Hing Kee where she witnessed business transactions daily rather than enjoying a child's life of outdoors with playmates, toys, music and books. In addition, her mother, Chin Shee, often exasperated with her and depressed after several miscarriages, welcomed the birth of their second child, son Gin-gow, who was docile and obedient, which caused her to withdraw from Yuet-yung.

As a child, Yuet-yung spent much time with her father, watching him conduct business at a time of fierce anti-Chinese sentiment, which required a tough constitution. With him as a role model, she soon mirrored his attitude in dealing with people and situations. As a consequence, she developed a personality that leaned toward focusing on the outer world of people and things. She was all business, cold and calculating; never focused on inner thoughts of ideas and impressions; only on the present, not the future; and ignoring feelings when making decisions.

Yuet-yung, daughter of Lew Hing

Yuet-yung would become Lew Hing's eyes and ears in Chinatown, providing him with important information about the goings and comings in Chinatown. She was no-nonsense underneath a seemingly gentle exterior; like a cobra waiting for the right moment to strike. A family relative once described her as the only one of his children who had "balls" and if she were a man, she would have been more than capable to maintain the family fortune. Barely four-foot-seven, she used her size to full advantage. In public, she was often underestimated. She used her role as a woman to gather information on all the comings and goings in Chinatown and beyond. Involved in every important social organization in Chinatown, from the YWCA to leading the efforts to raise money for disaster relief in China and supporting the war bond effort in China, she was known as "Dai Gu" or Big Aunt.

For Quan Yeen, becoming cold and calculating came after he assumed responsibility for running Mu Tin. Born in Fresno in 1878 to Quan Ying Nung and Tom Shee, he was destined to be a third-generation merchant in the family business, a high-end dry goods wholesaling company started by his grandfather, Quan Shi Jiao, in San Francisco.

Quan Yeen, son-in-law to Lew Ying, as a youth in Fresno

The son of a Sam Yup merchant, Quan Cheng Chang, in Canton, Quan Shi Jiao and his wife and baby Ying Nung were dispatched to San Francisco in 1854 to establish a branch of the family company. Ying Nung grew up comfortably in Chinatown, attending a missionary school with other young men of rich Sam Yup Chinese merchants who wanted their sons to be able to transact business with the whites.

When the railroad to Fresno was completed in 1872, many Chinese went to the central valley to farm. To provide goods to the newly settled Chinese, Quan Shi Jiao sent Quan Ying Nung and his new bride to open a branch of the dry goods store in San Francisco. There, both Quan Yeen and his older brother, Quan Poon, were born.

In 1885, Quan Shi Jiao needed to return to China, summoned by his father, Quan Cheng Chang, now in his seventies, to run the family export business in Canton. Quan Shi Jiao then summoned Quan Ying Nung, his wife and eldest son, Quan Poon, to San Francisco to run the family business on Dupont Street. Before they left, Quan Ying Nung met with his white business attorney, Milius King Harris, with whom he had developed a personal friendship beyond a lawyer-client relationship.

Quan Ying Nung: *"Milius, I have been summoned to San Francisco by my father to run the family business in San Francisco. We would like to keep this branch in Fresno open but my son Quan Yeen is only seven. Can we work out an arrangement where my son can live with your family as a houseboy and be able to learn English and American ways? In exchange, if you supervise my business interests for which Quan Yeen can help as a translator, I will share the profits with you for your services."*

Milius King Harris: *"Ying Nung, let me speak with Mrs. Harris to see how we might be able to accommodate your request."*

Nine years later, in 1894, Quan Yeen left Fresno to rejoin his family in San Francisco. M.K. Harris continued to oversee the Quan business interests in Fresno Chinatown.

Married in 1898 to Lew Hing's daughter, he soon became a trusted compatriot of his father-in-law, particularly after his skillful handling of the Mu Tin organization. When the earthquake caused many refugees to settle in Oakland, Quan Yeen and fellow clansmen formed the Oakland branch of Loong Kong, extending the reach of Mu Tin and its activities to the now-growing Chinatown there.

Quan Yeen became quite familiar with the white authorities in Oakland and Alameda County, overseeing payoffs to protect the gambling and opium operations. Deputized to carry a gun by the Alameda County Sheriff, he would return to Oakland with a bodyguard, bringing money from the previous night's activities in San Francisco, and then personally

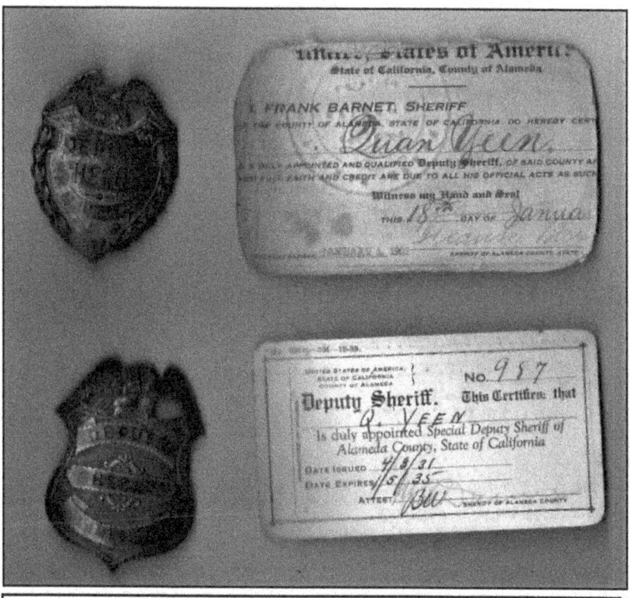

Quan Yeen's Deputy Sheriff badges and I.D.

picking up the money from the gambling houses and opium dens in Oakland in the evening. With his early exposure to American ways, he easily switched to impeccable English and western clothing, and was comfortable in the presence of white people.

Quan Yeen's admonition to the members associated with Mu Tin activities was to keep a low profile. However, events beyond his control brought unwanted publicity and attention to Mu Tin. It started with the discovery in 1909 of the body of a young white woman inside of a steamer trunk in a room of a member of Mu Tin in New York. Feeling their colleague had been ill-treated, the Four Brothers (as Mu Tin was known to the whites) came to his defense, putting the organization on the white authorities' watch list.

Then a more sensational case followed—the murder of Bow How, also involving Mu Tin. This incident ignited an open war between the Tongs and the Mu Tin. The war terrified the whites and tourism dropped precipitously with dire economic consequences for Chinatown. The war lasted over a year and even Six Companies and the Chinese Consul were powerless to stop it.

Finally, in 1910, a peace agreement was reached that bound both Mu Tin and the On Leong Tong. While specifically addressing the incident in New York, it also revealed the nationwide nature of the criminal organizations, as all branches nationwide were bound to honor the provisions that murderers were to be surrendered to the police, and blood retribution would be forsworn in favor of financial settlements achieved through mediation.

As a result, the authorities no longer considered Mu Tin as simply a clan organization, defending its members if they were treated unfairly; Mu Tin was now placed on a par with the Tongs. Quan Yeen had to spend time convincing the white authorities that Mu Tin would not needlessly cause trouble in Chinatown; his promises were backed up by spreading more money around, which helped to placate the authorities. In the late 1920s, Quan Yeen was appointed a Deputy Sheriff in Alameda County.

At the same time as the simmering tensions between Mu Tin and other Tongs, a bigger issue loomed in the minds of both the Chinese and whites—the struggle between the Manchu Dynasty and the Nationalist and Reformist Movements seeking to overthrow the Dynasty.

SEVEN

U. S. ATTITUDE TOWARDS CHINA

CHINESE REVOLUTION AND AMERICAN ATTITUDES TOWARDS CHINESE

1908-1912

Beginning in 1908, a new element, the fight between the Qing Dynasty and the nationalist and reformist movement in China, had begun to dominate the daily life of Chinatown. The Empress promised that China would transition to a constitutional government but the opposition wanted nothing short of an end to the dynasty. White America hoped for the continuation of the transition of the Qing Dynasty to a constitutional government for economic reasons. This excerpt from a essay commemorating the centennial of the revolution sums up the concerns:

> "...On the eve of revolution in October, 1911, the Qing Dynasty seemed headed in a direction favorable to American business interests, promising domestic stability, a smooth and willing transition to constitutional government, and above all a strong

and growing demand for American steel, machinery, and ships.

"Against that backdrop of economic engagement and the promise of stability, the republican revolution was a hard sell. The revolutionaries went to great lengths to project a pro-Western image, but Young China activists could not escape the menace of their association with anarchism and assassination. Ideologically, the revolutionaries in China could scarcely mask their resentment of the foreign powers —which lurked just behind their primary hatred of the Manchus. Spokesmen for the revolution outwardly promised no harm would come to foreign interests in China, but to their own followers the rhetoric was often different.

"Publications in Chinese were rife with venom against the western presence in China, and while Sun Yat-sun and others tried to keep such sentiments from foreign ears, the basic message could still slip out. *The New-York Tribune* reported such a speech in New York's Chinatown on October 22, 1911 by one Jue Check-man (whom the *Tribune's* article called the 'revolutionary apostle of Canton'), who attacked the dynasty's close ties to American business and threatened his audience that if the Manchus remained in power they would appoint JP Morgan China's minister of finance, and Andrew Carnegie her minister of war. It was hardly a message to endear him to American elites.

"They would warm up in time, once it came to seem inevitable, but on the eve of revolution Americans weren't impressed by the possibility of a republican government's being established in China.

The United States and the Manchu dynasty were close allies ... and the constitutional monarchy on offer from the Qing seemed a more stable foundation for a future state than some revolutionary republic....For beyond any questions of political

Racist Cartoon: The Yellow Peril in all his Glory

structure and domestic order for China's own sake, the prospect of revolution tapped into a darker and more subtle concern abroad: that a racially unified, modernizing China might threaten the dominance of the West.

"Though Europeans and Americans originally used the term "Yellow Peril" to describe Japan, which after its defeat of China in 1895 and Russia in 1905 had proven itself a world-class military power, by the time of the 1911 revolution they were applying it to China as well. Looking back to the Boxers, and forward from the 1911 Revolution, some saw a different kind of Yellow Peril emerging from China—namely, that if 400 million Chinese should throw off the shackles of Manchu oppression and unite, there was no telling what revenge they might wreak on the foreign powers that had helped the Manchus keep them under control.

"The attempted assassination of Prince Zaixun on September 29,1910 by George Fong, a native born American when he arrived in San Francisco on his way to see the U.S. President had brought home the message that America's Chinatowns were crucibles of revolution, and as the violence in China unfolded, American observers were both bemused and disturbed by the presence of "Young China" in their own midst—indeed, several seemed convinced that the whole Chinese revolution was in fact being directed from within the United States.

"The *San Francisco Chronicle* predicted that "it will be recorded that San Francisco's Chinatown was the starting point for one of the greatest political movements, ancient or modern." The New-York Tribune went further, declaring that "San Francisco will go down in the history of nations as the mother of the new Chinese republic." It wasn't exactly a point of pride, though; the new Chinese state was going to be born, in their eyes, from a site of "the bloody tong wars; down where the powerful kings of the opium ring held out for decades; down where the Chinese traffickers in slant-eyed slave girls conducted their nefarious work year in and year out."[37]

Demonstrators in SF Chinatown, c. 1910

In 1910 in San Francisco, the revolutionary Sun Yat-sen established the radical T'ung Meng Hui, the forerunner to the Chinese Nationalist Party. He also founded the *Young China Daily* which along with three other Chinatown newspapers served as an exiled journalistic organ advocating the overthrow of the Manchus. A politicized population in half-exile—that is what Chinatown often meant. Another excerpt from the same essay lays out the issues:

> "This consistent undercurrent of political activity is an important subtext to the redevelopment of Chinatown.

[37] Stephen Platt, *The "United States of China." 100 Years Later,* (Essay) December 20, 2011. Chinafile.com

"In an odd confluence, political dissent was nurtured within the increasingly consumer-friendly tourist quarter. The 1911 October Revolution which effectively ended three hundred years of Manchu rule in China, was almost completely financed by overseas Chinese; that is tuxedoed merchants helped to fund an entire overthrow…

"With Glitter Chinatown, the possibility that a founding opposition in radical behavior, between an embrace of activist politics and an embrace of a tourist industry, was at one time not held to be so reducible. Young radicalized Chinese men attempted to include, rather than repress or discard, the products and desires of the American commodity fetish.

"In the case of young, immigrant men, the spectacle of Chinatown, with its precious porcelains, silk brocades, asphalt streets, and electric lamps, was a space still in the making. The self-conscious fabrication of a consumerized ethnic subculture was a way of elaborating a nationalist political stance. Categorizing, displaying, and selling the industrialized kitsch products of the Chinese was a means by which to articulate a nationalist identity from a distance.

"'Dr. Sun had told us that our main job in America was to raise funds,' a young revolutionary once observed.. To fight, he became a dry goods clerk, peddling Chinese goods to the quarter's new visitors. In the early development of touristic Chi-

> natown, the collected objects and colorful environment inspired a collective wish-image for the nation-state."[38]

While the overseas Chinese viewed the Qing government as weak and corrupt and unable to protect them from white countries, the whites continued the virulent racist perception of the Chinese and were fearful of retribution from a republican government.

> "The menace of the Chinatowns was one thing, but the menace of China itself was another—and in 1911 the nation that appeared on the verge of rising to power in Asia had good reason to be angry. The Americans and British were hardly unaware of the questionable morality of their policies in China over the previous century—few in either country would argue that opium had been unharmful to China, the gunboat treaties fair, or the indemnities affordable. Thus, the Chinese national form of the Peril rested on an acknowledgement that if China did harbor a grudge against the West, it was, given the circumstances of history, justified. "Let us hope," said the *Chicago Tribune* when it learned that the Qing emperor had abdicated, "that the yellow peril will never be as perilous to white people as the white peril has been to the yellow people."
>
> "It is no coincidence that the Western literary archetype of China's Yellow Peril, the evil Dr. Fu

[38] Foundsf.org. *Chinese Nationalism.*_Excerpted from *Reclaiming San Francisco: History, Politics, Culture,* A City Lights Anthology, 1998.

> Manchu, made his first appearance soon after the 1911 Revolution...."[39]

Chinese responded in kind to the continued characterization of the Chinese as the "yellow peril." Sentiments against the whites could be found in the holding barracks on Angel Island in San Francisco Bay where imprisoned would-be immigrants carved their hopes for the new China into the walls.

> "If there comes a day when China will be united," wrote one, "I will surely cut out the heart and bowels of the western barbarian."
>
> "Wrote another: "I strongly advise my countrymen not to worry, Even though you are imprisoned in a wooden building, Someday after China rises and changes, She will be adept at using bombs to obliterate America."
>
> "But the feared payback for China's 19th century humiliations never did come. The Republic of China quickly collapsed without unifying the country in any lasting fashion, and so the time never arrived when its government might demand an end to foreign concessions or drive unwanted foreign interest from the country. The moment passed, the threat—if there even was one—subsided, and business continued as before."[40]

In 1912, Charles M. Schwab, then President of Bethlehem Steel, opined in an interview that the real "Yellow Peril" was going to be industrial rather than military, that Americans

---

[39] Stephen A. Platt, *"The United States of China." 100 Years Later,* (Essay) December 20, 2011, Chinafile.com

[40] Ibid., *"The United States of China," 100 Years Later."*

should not fear war from a modernized China but competition. But he ended his interview by reassuring his audience at that time not to worry because "it will be more than a century before China becomes an industrial peril."[41]

And more to the point, the *San Francisco Chronicle* in May, 1911 reported before the revolution:

> "Contemplating the diligence, sobriety and cleverness of the Chinese, in connection with their immense numbers and their low standard of comfort, some foresee a manufacturing China, turning out great quantities of iron, steel, implements, ships, machinery and textiles at an incredibly low cost, and thereby driving our goods out of neutral markets and obliging our workingmen, after a long, disastrous strike with their employers, to take a Chinese wage or starve."

How prescient!

A GREATER PRESENCE IN CHINATOWN 1906 - 1915

Despite his success with the Pacific Coast Canning venture, Lew Hing realized in an atmosphere of anti-Chinese sentiment, his business ventures in the outside white world were always one step from disaster. For this reason, from 1905 to 1919, he balanced investing in businesses reliant on the white consumers—Pacific Coast Cannery, Bayside Cannery in Alviso, Bayside Fish Cannery in Monterey, Chinese-Mexican Mercantile Company and Wah Muck Cotton Plantation in Mexicali, Mexico—with business ventures in Chinatown— Sing Chong and Nanjing Fook Wah Import/Export,

[41] Ibid., *"The United States of China," 100 Years Later."*

the Republic Hotel and Mun Ming Lue Kwan hotels, and Hop Wo Cheung in Canton and Hop Wo Lung in San Francisco, wholesale food and dry goods distributors. In addition, he was an investor and later President of the Canton Bank and Chairman of the Board of the China Mail Steamship Company.[42]

In 1911, just four months before the Qing government fell, he was appointed a director to Six Companies. He would remain a director until 1927. In this position, he participated in the governance of Chinatown.

He also became a major benefactor in Chinatown, including donating funds for the construction of the swimming pool at the YMCA (which was named for him), the rebuilding of the Four Family Association building, and contributions to the building fund for the new Chinese hospital.

YMCA Groundbreaking Ceremony, November 15, 1924.
In the center is Robert Dollar, lumber baron and shipping magnate; to his left is Lew Hing.

[42] For a complete list of Lew Hing's businesses and investments, see Appendix A of this book.

A BENEFICIAL RELATIONSHIP 1903-1923

From 1903 to 1923, future San Francisco Mayor "Sunny Jim" Rolph and his brother William Rolph benefited in significant ways from their relationship with Lew Hing.

The Rolphs were appreciative of the profits flowing into their coffers from the Pacific Canning Company as it continued to operate while its competitors, whose plants were in San Francisco, hastened to rebuild after the earthquake. The Rolphs were also appreciative of Lew Hing's foresight to locate the cannery next to the railhead. It made selling the products of Pacific Coast Cannery across the country much easier than if the cannery had been built by a port or inland away from easy transport.

Every morning, Lew Hing would spend the morning at the cannery in Oakland, then take the ferry with his bodyguard to Chinatown to check on matters there. For protection, he had chosen a suite in the Republic Hotel on Grant Avenue as his office. It was a safe choice as members of Mu Tin could congregate in the lobby to protect both Lew Hing and Quan Yeen. When Hop Wo Lung, the dry goods business opened by Lew Hing in 1895 originally at 716 Commercial Street before the earthquake, was reopened at 718 Grant Avenue, two doors down from the hotel entrance, Quan Yeen became the general manager and thc storefront doubled as the headquarters of Mu Tin.

After meetings in Chinatown, Lew Hing would spend the afternoon at the Rolph Company. Often taking lunch with William Rolph, they became good friends. When James Rolph entered politics, Abe Ruef was the city boss of San Francisco. At a time when California was the center of corruption, influenced by the Southern Pacific Railroad, which controlled both political parties in the state, many of these wealthy and powerful people lived in San Francisco. When necessary, these power brokers reinforced their hold on power through corrupt politicians and city bosses.

Ruef chose E. E. Schmitz to run for Mayor in 1902 and when elected as the Union Labor Party candidate, his administration, while remaining popular with the working class, gave protection to criminals, including houses of prostitution, for protection money. Later, Schmitz was found guilty of extortion in 1907; in a separate trial, Boss Ruef was found guilty of bribery. Fed up with the corruption, the ruling class asked Rolph, who had risen in the ranks of the Democratic Party, to run for Mayor in 1909. He declined then, but ran successfully in 1911. This was the event Lew Hing had hoped for to realize his dream.

Lew Hing's banquet in honor of Mayor Rolph's election at Hung Fa Low, the fanciest restaurant in San Francisco Chinatown. L to R at head table: William Rolph, James Rolph, Sr., Lew Hing, Mayor Rolph and Mrs. Rolph, the Consul General of the Republic of China.

ALIEN LAND LAWS

1913

By 1913, with Pacific Coast Cannery, The Canton Bank and Hop Wo Lung on firm footing, Lew Hing looked for more opportunities. Flushed with cash and wanting to put it to use, he tried to find ways to either acquire or lease available land which was plentiful. As an immigrant ineligible for naturalization, he was barred from directly purchasing land by the California constitution of 1879. In the midst of anti-Chinese sentiment in 1879, the California legislature had rewritten its constitution, claiming to follow the federal 1870 Naturalization Act, which removed the "white-only" restriction on citizenship which had been in force since 1790, and expanded naturalization rights to anyone of African descent. With this definition, if a person was neither white nor of African American descent, they were not eligible for naturalization. California masked its racism as limiting the rights of Chinese immigrants, like Lew Hing, without targeting them specifically in the language of the law.

Nearly 35 years later, the same stench of racism permeated the hall of the Capitol when the California legislature enacted the Alien Land Act of 1913. Passed during the anti-Japanese hysteria, the law prohibited aliens ineligible for citizenship from possessing long-term land leases.

California further tightened the economic noose on immigrants when in 1920 it passed an amendment to the 1913 Alien Land Act prohibiting even short-term leases of land to aliens ineligible for citizenship. This amendment was based on arguments by anti-Japanese groups, echoing the anti-Chinese rhetoric, that Japanese were a threat to economic competition, and that they were incapable of fully assimilating into American society.

The highest court of the land, the U.S. Supreme Court, affirmed the rights of states to pass discriminatory laws. "Even though the issue of citizen property ownership complicated rulings, the U.S. Supreme Court ruled in 1923 the laws restricting the rights of aliens ineligible for citizenship from owning land directly were not a violation of aliens' rights to equal protection under the 14th Amendment"[43]

Ownership or control of land was the main method of accumulating wealth in the United States and the effect of the legislation in California as well as surrounding states like Oregon and Washington and affirmation ultimately by the Supreme Court at the time all but cut off an avenue for Lew Hing to build sustainable wealth.

It was only as recently as the middle of the twentieth century that the U.S. Supreme Court, perhaps sensing the injustice perpetrated by the alien land laws, began ruling against alien land laws, upholding the rights of citizens first to hold property despite their relationship with alien parents ineligible for citizenship, and later determining that alien land laws did infringe on aliens' rights to equal protection under the law.[44] Finally, in 1952, the California Supreme Court invalidated the remaining alien land laws in the case of Sei Fuji v. California when it determined that forbidding aliens from owning land was a violation of the 14th Amendment's equal protection clause.[45]

[43] Porterfield v. Webb, 263 U.S. 225; Webb v. O'Brien, 263 U.S. 313; Frick v. Webb, 263 U.S. 326; Terrace v. Thompson, 263 U.S. 197 (1923)

[44] Oyama v. California, 332 U.S. 633 (1948)

[45] Sei Fuji v. California, 242 P.2d 617 (1952).

LEW HING INVESTS IN MEXICO: CHINESE-MEXICAN MERCANTILE COMPANY

1913

With Chinese immigration to the United States barred by the 1882 Exclusion Act, Imperial China looked for other countries for bilateral agreements. In 1899, Mexico and China signed the treaty of amity and commerce providing for free and voluntary movement by the citizens of two countries. Chinese immigrants were also entitled to all rights accorded nationals of other foreign countries, including owning land and their own businesses.

Rejected by a hostile regime in the United States amid a tide of xenophobia, migrant workers fled south of the border in search of opportunities. They were not Mexican, but Chinese. There, they established an agriculture industry that still thrives. The origin of Mexicali was described by Mya Gilber in her paper addressing the forbidden history of the Chinese in Mexico:

> "In 1902, a syndicate of Los Angeles businessmen organized the Colorado River Land Company (CRLC), and acquired nearly 850,000 acres if the Mexicali Valley. Throughout the early twentieth century, the Mexican government attempted to resettle Mexican families in Baja California in order to integrate the region more closely with the rest of the country. Unfortunately, resettlement plans consistently failed to attract Mexican settlers, as better opportunities were just across the border.
>
> "The Chinese that founded Mexicali, now the capital of Baja California, 'were intimately involved in every phase of land reclamation and farm-making', according to historian Jason Oliver.

> Without them, he says, 'it would have taken decades longer to develop into one of the richest agricultural areas in the world.'
>
> "Chinese expertise in cotton cultivation allowed them to transform the desert border area into an irrigated colony by channeling water from the Colorado River. The irrigation system functions to this day and sustains abundant agricultural activity....
>
> The distinctive development of northern Baja enabled the Chinese to assume diverse economic roles, ranging from rural laborers to urban capitalists. Strong demand for labor coupled with low native competition, provided ideal conditions for the new immigrants. There were so many Chinese-owned stores that, in the local language, *to go to the store* was to visit 'el chino on the corner.' Yet, despite a highly visible Chinese presence, Mexican residents had high opinions of Chinese businesses, as they often allowed people to purchase on credit. The newspaper *El Excelsior* noted that Mexicali was 'an entirely Chinese city. The streets, traveled only by Chinese, the restaurants filled by Chinese, the fieldwork absolutely dominated by Chinese. Everything, everywhere is completely Chinese in Mexicali.'"[46]

By 1909, with the Inter-California Railway linking towns in the Mexicali Valley to Southern Pacific's railroad

[46] Mya Gelber, *Los Chinos de la Chinsea: Destabilizing Natural Narratives and Uncovering the Forgotten History of the Chinese in Mexico,* 2018. digitalcommons.bard.edu.

network in California, CRLC decided to turn the Mexicali Valley into a main cotton-growing region.

When CRLC encountered a shortage of laborers, CRLC started importing Chinese laborers directly from Chinese port cities like Hong Kong and Shanghai through Chinese middlemen. The middlemen were responsible for delivering the laborers to the dock in Hong Kong. CRLC and Southern Pacific, both connected politically at the state and federal level, used their influence to circumvent the 1882 Exclusion Act. Pacific Mail Steamship Lines, owned by Southern Pacific, with lines traveling from Hong Kong to San Francisco, carried Chinese laborers who, through a federal waiver program, disembarked in San Francisco where they were processed through immigration. Then, under guard, the laborers were immediately put on a Southern Pacific train to Calexico where a temporary immigration station was set up to process them through to Mexicali. The first of many groups, a party of 51, arrived in February 1910.

Chinese agricultural labor became the only practical alternative to meet the demand in a depleted labor market that faced chronic shortages. By 1919, 50 Chinese-owned cotton farms came to occupy almost 75,000 acres, producing 80 percent of the cotton grown in the Mexicali Valley. Once the irrigation and clearing projects were completed, over 10,000 Chinese congregated in a section of Mexicali now known as La Chinsea.

In April 1913, the *Calexico Chronicle* reported that three Chinese businessmen—Lim Kim Tuck, Wong Fook Yee and Dr. S.A. Wong—were in Mexicali looking for a site to build a large grocery and supply store. They were familiar with Mexico as they had already invested in a cantaloupe farm in Mexico in Baja, California in early 1913.

The three businessmen, not having the reputation or stature within the Chinese community to successfully attract investment, turned to Lew Hing. Lim Kim Tuck knew Lew Hing as he had been a partner in Lew Hing's Hop Wo Chong wholesale store in Hong Kong.

They met with Lew Hing and, emphasizing the growing community of Chinese in Mexicali because CRLC was importing more and more Chinese laborers to work the increasing acreage of cotton, they pitched the opportunity for Pacific Coast Cannery, Hop Wo Chong and Hop Wo Lung to supply the goods to be sold in the store.

In May 1913, Lew Hing circulated a prospectus to form the new business in Mexicali. The three partners hoped that Lew Hing's stature in the Chinese community would help in

Mercantil Chino-Mexicali building

realizing their vision. The prospectus listed Lew Hing as the "plenipotentiary president", the person authorized to receive the investment.

The project was quickly fully subscribed and moved forward with the building of the first permanent building in the heart of Mexicali just across the street from the railway station and three blocks from the Heffernan Avenue border crossing in Calexico. By the fall of 1913, Wa Muck opened its doors. The operation was sizable as the *Calexico Chronicle* noted in August 1, 1913, even before the building was completed, two carloads of goods—5,111 pieces of dry goods, groceries and furniture for which over $5,000 in duty was paid—had been delivered.

The new venture proved profitable for Lew Hing's Pacific Coast Cannery and Hop Wo Chong and Hop Wo Lung as they were the major suppliers of the dry goods and groceries for the store and later for the Canton Bank which gained more business by processing remittances by the growing number of workers in Mexicali to their families in China.

THE PANAMA CANAL AND THE PANAMA PACIFIC INTERNATIONAL EXPOSITION

1915

In Lew Hing's lifetime, there would be two major transportation events which would dramatically transform the United States. As major an event as the completion of the transcontinental railroad was in 1869 to the United States, the completion of the Panama Canal 45 years later in 1914 was even more economically transforming, opening up Asia to the East Coast and Europe to the West Coast. Conceived and started in 1882, it would take more than 30 years to complete.

The rush of settlers to California and Oregon in the mid-nineteenth century was the initial impetus in the United States to build an artificial waterway across Central America to connect the Atlantic and Pacific Oceans. Construction had begun in 1881 but earlier attempts by the French company which had completed the Suez Canal failed. By the turn of the century, sole possession of the isthmian canal became imperative to the United States, which had acquired an overseas empire at the end of the Spanish-American War. The United States needed the ability to move warships and commerce quickly between the Atlantic and Pacific oceans. After years of political problems were resolved, construction began in 1909. On August 15, 1914, the Panama Canal was opened to traffic.

When the United States took over control of canal construction in 1903, San Francisco city leaders envisioned San Francisco as host of a grand international exposition commemorating the completion of the Panama Canal. The earthquake and fire of 1906 gave momentum to the idea of hosting a World's Fair. Ostensibly to celebrate the completion of the canal, more importantly, to the city and California, it was intended to replace in the eyes of the world the image of a destroyed San Francisco.

Mayor Rolph realized the importance of successfully staging the fair, called the Panama Pacific International Exposition (PPIE) and took a leading role from its inauguration, assuming the position as Vice President of the Exposition to ensure that the city government fully committed its resources.

One afternoon, when Lee Hing arrived at the Rolph Company offices, he found the Mayor waiting for him.

Mayor Rolph: *"Hing, it's good to see you again. William has constantly reported on how successful our relationship with Pacific Coast Canning has been. I apologize for not seeing you earlier but I've been too busy cleaning up the city."*

Lew Hing: *"Mr. Mayor, first congratulations on your election and wishing you many positive achievements."*

Mayor Rolph: *"Hing, this is the reason for my visit today. The upcoming World's Fair is very important to San*

Francisco. If we successfully stage the event, it is sure to increase tourism, investment and spur development, cementing California as the trade gateway between Europe and Asia through the canal. China has just undergone a difficult period and as such an important trading partner of the United States, it is vital that it has a presence at the fair."

Lew Hing: *"What would you ask me to do for you, Mr. Mayor?"*

Mayor Rolph: *"You are well respected as the leading merchant in the Chinese community, you can tell the new leaders of China that this Fair is an important place to show the world that its commercial ties are still strong and will honor all contracts with the international community."*

Lew Hing: *"I will do my best to contact the proper authorities and report back to you."*

Mayor Rolph: *"Thank you, Hing."*

The irony of Mayor Rolph's request was it was made against a backdrop of fierce anti-Chinese and anti-Asian sentiment in San Francisco and California. Indeed, the effort to pass the 1913 Alien Land Act was led by former Mayor Phelan of San Francisco and coining of the term "Yellow Peril" of the newspapers of W.R. Hearst reflected the racial hatred by whites in power at the time.

While the Chinese revolution in 1911 was successful in ousting the Manchu Dynasty, it failed to unify the country under its control. The Qing withdrawal led to a power vacuum in certain regions, resulting in the rise of warlords, often controlling their territories without acknowledging the nationalist government. In short, the request by the Mayor to Lew Hing was a challenge to accomplish.

Lew Hing was well aware of the sentiment of the white establishment but looked at this as an opportunity to gain favor with Mayor Rolph. The contacts Lew Hing's family had made by giving substantial funds sub-rosa to the nationalists, much of it from the vault in Oakland, opened the door to putting forth his inquiry through proper channels. When he had a response, another meeting with the Mayor was arranged.

Pleasantries aside, they got right down to business.

Lew Hing: *"The new government agrees that it needs to be at the Fair but at the moment, the coffers are bare. They have asked me to raise the funds to build the pavilion while they arrange for companies to send goods to be displayed."*

Mayor Rolph: *"I can't promise any funding as the budget is set and all the money raised has been committed but I can make sure that all materials and supplies for construction and furnishing the building can be greatly discounted."*

Lew Hing: *"The community has yet to fully recover from funding the revolution but we will endeavor to find sources of funds which might be available should the city cooperate."*

Mayor Rolph: *"I fully understand," well aware that gambling houses, opium dens and brothels were known to provide a tidy profit.*

Lew Hing then called a joint meeting of the Chinese Chamber of Commerce and Six Companies, and spoke to the members:

"Mayor Rolph has approached me and asked a favor, a favor which, if the Chinese community can deliver, will stand us in good stead with the city. Since the war in Europe has reduced the number of countries participating in the World's Fair, it is important that China be involved. He asked me to pursue the matter with the new Republic.

"Unfortunately, the Consul General says, the priority of the new government is uniting the country, so China can organize trade delegations to bring products to exhibit but the government has little money to build the building. I will pledge to raise money for this project by buying stock in the Panama Pacific Exposition Corporation, who will join me?"

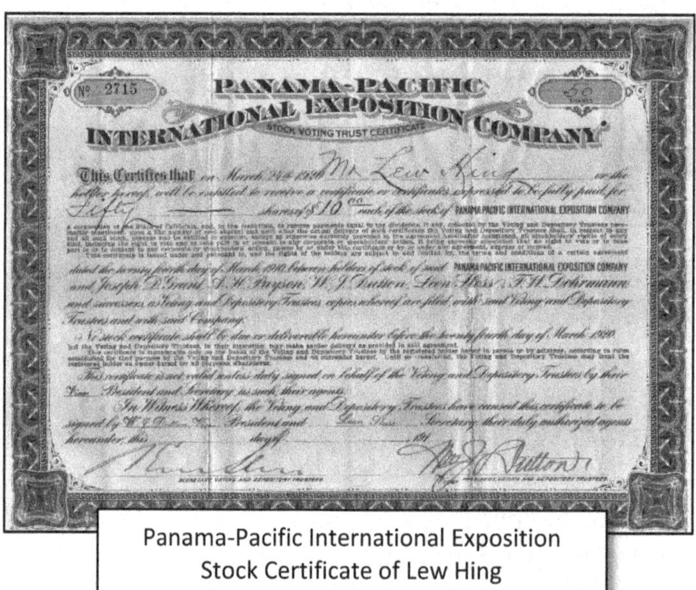

No 2715 | 50

PANAMA-PACIFIC INTERNATIONAL EXPOSITION COMPANY

STOCK VOTING TRUST CERTIFICATE

This Certifies that on March 24th 1920 Mr Lew Hing or the holder hereof, will be entitled to receive a certificate or certificates expressed to be fully paid for Fifty shares of $10 each of the stock of PANAMA PACIFIC INTERNATIONAL EXPOSITION COMPANY

dated the twenty fourth day of March, 1910 between holders of stock of said PANAMA PACIFIC INTERNATIONAL EXPOSITION COMPANY and Joseph D. Grant, A. H. Payson, W. J. Dutton, Leon Sloss, F. W. Dohrmann and successors as Voting and Depository Trustees copies whereof are filed with said Voting and Depository Trustees and with said Company.

No stock certificate shall be due or deliverable hereunder before the twenty fourth day of March 1920

This certificate is not valid unless duly signed on behalf of the Voting and Depository Trustees by their Vice President and Secretary as such their agents.

In Witness Whereof, the Voting and Depository Trustees have caused this certificate to be signed by W. J. Dutton Vice President and Leon Sloss Secretary, their duly authorized agents hereunder, this day of 191

Panama-Pacific International Exposition
Stock Certificate of Lew Hing

Lew Hing met with the Mayor once again: *"Mr. Mayor, as a pledge that our community will raise the funds to build the Republic of China Pavilion, here is a list of leading merchants who have purchased stock in the corporation, demonstrating our commitment to the success of the event."*

The Republic of China Pavilion was successfully built, engendering goodwill between the Mayor and the Chinese community. The real winner was Lew Hing. He walked away with a favor from the Mayor in his pocket and greater respect in Chinatown.

However, when the Exposition opened in February of 1915, the Joy Zone, the entertainment portion of the exposition, revealed a darker side where racial prejudices were on

Pavilion of the Republic of China at the PPIE.

full display. Using racial stereotypes as a marketing tool, the concessionaires bargained on sensationalism, depicting other cultures in a way to imply white superiority. One particularly offensive booth was called "Underground Chinatown", allegedly focusing on stereotypical depictions of

Chinese culture, such as an opium den, complete with wax figures and opium pipes. This caused such a great uproar among the local Chinese community that Lew Hing and the Consul General of China met with Mayor Rolph to ask that the booth be closed down. That didn't happen; however, the name was changed to "Underground Slumming" and all the Chinese wax figures were removed from the display.

A BOOST TO THE BOTTOM LINE

1914-1918

When war broke out in Europe in 1914, it overshadowed the news of completion of the Panama Canal and greatly dampened the world's participation in the upcoming Panama Pacific International Exposition planned for the next year. The war did, however, bring prosperity to the Rolphs and Lew Hing and their respective businesses.

Herbert Hoover, a mining engineer and financier, was living in London at the outbreak of the war. He was among tens of thousands of American tourists trying to get home. They were stuck without financial resources to return to America as their paper securities and travelers checks were not accepted, and most had little hard currency to buy passage on ships.

Hoover had previously experienced being part of a trapped group of foreigners. Caught in China during the Boxer Rebellion in 1900, he had displayed his gift for humanitarian rescue by organizing relief then. He drew on this experience now.

Hoover set up and organized a committee to get the Americans home, making loans and cashing checks as needed. By October 1914, some 120,000 Americans reached home and in the end, there remained just $300 in unpaid debt.

Hoover's talents did not go unnoticed, as the American Ambassador to the United Kingdom and other key people in London sought him out for a bigger problem, feeding starving Belgians. A previous attempt to bring in food had failed and Hoover was contacted.

For the next three years, Hoover headed the Commission for Relief in Belgium (CRB) an international organization for the supply of food to German-occupied Belgium and northern France. The Commission's task was to obtain foodstuffs from abroad and ship them into Belgium. He called it "the greatest charity the world has ever seen" and exhibited impressive executive ability in helping to procure food for some nine million people whose country had been overrun by the German army.

Herbert Hoover (right), head of American Relief Administration for U.S. Government, 1914-17 *(Photo from WSJ/Opinion, English edition, October 17, 2014, article by G.H.Nash)*

Operating in the face of resentment from both of the warring sides, Hoover engaged in shuttle diplomacy, negotiating safe conduct terms in meetings with British and German authorities. The CRB became an independent "Republic of Relief" with its own flag, navy, factories, mills and railroads. Private donations and government grants supplied an $11-million-a-month budget.

Hoover had known Mayor Rolph from the time Hoover stayed in the Bay Area. Through the Rolphs, Pacific Coast Cannery became a vendor, shipping its Buckskin Brand canned fruits and vegetables, featuring a logo with the likeness of Buffalo Bill Cody, to Europe. The completion of the Panama Canal made possible transport of goods from the West Coast in a reasonable time. In the end, CRB shipped 11.4 billion pounds of food to 9.5 million civilians.

Pacific Coast Cannery and the James Rolph Company made a lot of money.

CHINA MAIL STEAMSHIP LINES

1915

In 1912, federal legislation prevented railroads from using the nearly completed Panama Canal, causing Southern Pacific Railroad to shut down Pacific Mail Steamship Company and sell its ships to the Grace Line, leaving Japan's Toyo Kisen Kaisha line as the only merchant lines between China and San Francisco.

On January 18, 1915, the Japanese government claimed special privileges in China during World War I. Because of these demands, the Chinese boycotted Japanese businesses. They were not going to place themselves at the mercy of a Japanese shipping line.

Without an alternative, a group of Chinese merchants, including Lew Hing, President of Pacific Coast Cannery, and Look Tin Eli, President of the Canton Bank, and others from the Chinese Chamber of Commerce, met to create the China Mail Steamship Lines. They agreed to invest in new shipping lines and asked Lew Hing to confer with Mayor Rolph who had contacts with shipping lines.

Business Report of China Mail Steamship Co.

Through discussions, China Mail Steamship Company was able to purchase the oldest, slowest and smallest of the Pacific Mail's ships for $300,000. In 1915, Mayor Rolph sat on the platform at the ship christening ceremony as Lew Hing's youngest daughter, Rose, performed the christening of the *SS China.*

When the Southern Pacific shut down its shipping lines, the Colorado River Land Company had no way to obtain Chinese labor from Hong Kong and Shanghai for the Mexicali cotton fields. While no records exist, it is believed that China Mail entered into an agreement to supply the workers from Hong Kong and China to San Francisco, where Southern Pacific continued to transport the workers from San Francisco to Mexicali under some contractual arrangement with CRLC. This continued service helped contribute to the financial success in the early days of China Mail.

Needing to expand to meet increasing demand for shipping of passengers and cargo in 1917, China Mail attempted to find an additional seaworthy ship. However, as all were in use in World War I, Look Tin Eli, then president of China Mail, convinced its board to purchase the *SS Congress*, a burned-out wreck from Pacific Coast Steamship Company,

Lew Hing's youngest daughter, Rose Lew, christens a China Mail ship, with Mayor Jim Rolph present (front row, center), 1915.

for $600,000. Eventually rendered seaworthy at the cost of $2 million it was relaunched as the *SS Nanking*. The rebuilt ship carried 123 first-class, 100 cabin-class and 154 steerage passengers to make 23 round trips. White passengers and some wealthy Chinese merchants were in first-class; cabin-class customers were mostly Chinese males and students; all steerage passengers were Chinese. The ship operated under white officers.

By 1919, China Mail purchased a third ship, the *SS Nile,* attesting to the popularity of China Mail with the traveling public.

THE PANCHO VILLA EPISODE

In February 1913, a military coup took place in the Mexican capital led by General Victoriano Huerta, the military commander of the city, and supported by the United States ambassador. President Francisco Madero was arrested and a short time later assassinated along with his vice-president, José María Pino Suárez, on 22 February 1913, following the series of events known as the Ten Tragic Days (*la Decena Trágica*). In death, Madero became a unifying force of disparate elements in Mexico opposed to the regime of Huerta. In the north, governor of Coahuila, Venustiano Carranza, led what became the Constitutionalist Army against Huerta, and ousted him in July 1914. The U.S. government announced its support of the Carranza government, and Pancho Villa, a revolutionary, was incensed.

Pancho Villa

On March 16, 1916, Pancho Villa crossed over the border and attacked the town of Columbus, New Mexico and the U.S. Army Camp Furlong, killing American citizens and soldiers and making off with horses, guns and ammunition. In response, President Wilson ordered the Army to chase him down. General Funston ordered General Pershing, commandant at Fort Bliss, to assemble an expeditionary force of 10,000 troops to enter Mexico to find and neutralize Villa.

At this time, the Chinese Mexican Mercantile Company was one of the larger accounts for Pacific Coast Cannery. William Rolph asked his brother Mayor Rolph to contact Pershing to offer to supply the troops from Mexicali. Mayor Rolph was friendly with Pershing as they socialized while he was the commandant of the Presidio in San Francisco. When his wife and three daughters were tragically killed in a fire at their home in the Presidio in 1915, Pershing had requested reassignment to Fort Bliss in Texas.

General Pershing

Rolph spoke with Pershing's lieutenant in charge of logistics who was trying to figure out how to supply the troops in the field. Unlike conventional warfare, chasing Villa would involve guerrilla warfare and affect how troops would be resupplied. Complicating matters was Carranza's refusal to allow the United States to use the Mexican rail system, as he did not want to appear to be a puppet of the United States. The lieutenant told Rolph that the provisions would need to be carried by trucks, and that the supplier would have to deliver the provisions to wherever they were required.

If they wanted the business, James Rolph Company and Pacific Coast Cannery needed to find a transportation solution, namely finding guards and drivers. Lew Hing thought about how to fashion a solution. There were still mercenaries from the Chinese Revolution in China who could be recruited and transported via the arrangements already serving the cotton farms in Mexicali. There also needed to be a warehouse or space in Mexicali to house the mercenaries and store the provisions.

Taking advantage of the exigencies, the U.S. government and The Chinese-Mexican Mercantile Company (Wah Muck) entered into an agreement to provision the troops.

James Rolph Company would arrange for delivery of the requested provisions and supplies from the Pacific Coast Cannery and other sources to Mexicali, and Lew Hing would provide some 400 former mercenaries from the Chinese Revolution to guard and transport the provisions to destinations specified by the U.S. Army in trucks supplied by the Army.

As additional compensation, the U.S. agreed that it would purchase the entire 1916 harvest of the Wah Muck Jick San Yuen cotton farm and lease from Wah Muck three blocks in Mexicali for a storage and distribution center and sleeping quarters for the guards and truck drivers.

By 1916, Lew Hing's vision of a vertically integrated business empire started to take shape through his many ownership and management positions: as president of the Canton Bank; owner of a fruit and vegetable ranch in Winters, California producing fruits and vegetables for Pacific Coast Cannery of which he was president; principal owner of Hop Wo Chong, a wholesale export operation in Hong Kong; general manager of Hop Wo Lung, wholesale operation in San Francisco and Oakland Chinatown; vice president and chairman of the board of China Mail Steamship Lines; president of Chinese-Mexican Mercantile Company in Mexicali; president of Kung Wo, developer and majority owner of Republic Hotel; developer and majority owner of Mun Ming Lue Kwan Hotel; majority owner of Nanjing Fook Wah import/export store; and major investor in Sing Chong Bazaar. He was also an investor in other businesses in San Francisco Chinatown. Through these businesses, he provided banking, transportation, housing services, food and dry goods and household goods to both Chinese and whites.

THE PERSHING CHINESE STORY

Pershing divided his force into two columns to seek out Pancho Villa, and made his main base encampment at Casas Grandes, Chihuahua. The truck-train system, so called as it consisted of a long group of trucks to convoy supplies to the encampment, strained the Quartermasters Corps' ability to effectively supply the troops. Fortunately Pershing was alerted to the potential difficulties of supporting troops in the mountainous desert region of Northern Mexico through his experience of chasing Moros in the southern Philippines through mountainous jungle terrain. And, expecting no cooperation from the Carranza government, Pershing and his staff knew they might need to make contingency plans to address the lack of support personnel by either using civilians or sacrificing troop strength to bolster the supply function.

Preparation for the campaign included relying on Chinese mercenaries for delivery of the provisions and other supplies; these men became known as the "Pershing Chinese."

Failing to capture Villa, the bulk of American forces were withdrawn in January 1917. Pershing publicly claimed the expedition a success, although privately he complained to family that President Wilson had imposed too many restrictions, which made it impossible for him to fulfill his mission. He admitted to having been "outwitted and outbluffed at every turn," and later wrote, "when the true history is written, it will not be a very inspiring chapter for school children, or even grownups to contemplate. Having dashed into Mexico with the intention of eating the Mexicans raw, we returned back at the first repulse and are now sneaking home under cover, like a whipped cur with its tail between its legs."[47]

When General Pershing withdrew from Mexico, 2,700 refugees accompanied the troops, of which 127 were Chinese. Leaving behind the 400 Chinese men brought over to guard and truck the supplies from Mexicali to his camps, Lew Hing notified Consul General T. K. Fong that their lives were in danger and he needed to negotiate their entry into the United States. T.K. Fong traveled from San Francisco to lead the group to the U.S. border in July 1917 where he negotiated their entry. Once in the United States, they were confined at Fort Sam Houston for the duration of World War I, and put to work in a variety of capacities supporting the war effort.

After the war, having no further need for their services, the government threatened to deport the 400 Chinese men. However, a civilian adviser, Tracey Page, working tirelessly on their behalf for years, secured them permanent residency on November 23, 1921, when President Warren G. Harding signed Public Law No. 29. This law established a legal precedent in immigration law—the introduction of special consideration for immigrants escaping political persecution—later known as political asylum.

Released from Fort Sam Houston, the detainees scattered throughout the United States in search of work, or headed back to China. Those Chinese who initially crossed over with Pershing stayed in San Antonio to form the local Chinese community. Many of the mercenaries, single men recruited from Taishan, took a train back to the San Francisco Bay Area where Lew Hing, keeping the promise made

---

[47] West, Elizabeth, *Santa Fe: 400 Years, 400 Questions: Commemorating the 400th Anniversary of the Founding of Santa Fe, New Mexico in 1610*. 2012, Sunstone Press., p.13.

to them by Lew Chock Suey in China, provided work in leased space of an existing cannery and called the new operations the Westside Cannery. Because of fervent anti-Chinese sentiment, which included vandalism and attempts to burn down the cannery, the cannery personnel were housed within the cannery grounds and the property fenced with barbed wire. The 1930 census listed 179 single men at the cannery; there had been only one Chinese listed in the 1920 census.

HOOVER REDUX

So skilled was Hoover's performance as the head of the Committee for Relief in Belgium that President Woodrow Wilson appointed him the head of the United States Food Administration (USFA) during World War I. Relying primarily on voluntary cooperation by the American public, Hoover had won widespread support for "wheatless" and "meatless" days so that as much of the nation's agricultural output as possible could be sent to soldiers at the front.

Recognized by war's end as the "Great Engineer" who could organize resources and personnel to accomplish extraordinary acts of benevolence, Hoover was the natural choice to head the American Relief Administration (ARA). The ARA sent shiploads of food and other life-sustaining supplies to war-ravaged Europe, including Germany and Bolshevik Russia, during the famine in that country in 1921-23. He arranged for six million tons of food to be shipped to each of the European countries. The outreach to Soviet Russia garnered Hoover much criticism, but he defended his actions on humanitarian grounds, saying, "Twenty million people are starving. Whatever their politics, they shall be fed."[48]

The USFA contracted with Pacific Coast Cannery for delivery of its Buckskin canned goods to various countries from 1917 to 1923, resulting in a flood of profits to the cannery.

> "World War I brought greatly increased sales in the form of overseas exports, leading to an expansion of the Oakland plant. Major repairs and alterations in 1918 (permits #50072-3 and #43106) were done under special permission from the Non-war Construction Department of the Alameda County Division, State Council of Defense of California, 'making it possible to pack the usual quantity of canned fruits and vegetables, great portions of which are required by the U.S. government' [correspondence in building permit files]. The Pacific Coast Canning Co., known after 1930 as Pacific Coast Canners, Inc., disappears from city directories by 1938….[49]

The major alterations included replacing the original cannery complex north of 12th Street with a large two-story reinforced concrete building costing $100,000. This building contained canning equipment on both floors, as well as a cafeteria, lavatories, locker rooms and hospital; a south wing housing a boiler and box factory, sited on the vacated west end of 12th Street, was built concurrently.

---

48 American Relief Administration, Role of Hoover, Aid to USSR, Britannica.com.

49 *City of Oakland Historical Survey*, p.5.

EIGHT

THE FALL
1923 - 1926

Definition of "Chinaman's chance"
Slang, often offensive: the slightest or barest chance—
usually used in negative constructions, e.g.
"He hasn't a *Chinaman's chance* of winning."
—Merriam-Webster Dictionary

FICKLE WINDS OF FATE

James Rolph was as ambitious and driven as Lew Hing. When he started both Rolph Shipping Co. and the James Rolph Company, he was the new kid on the block, looking to establish his credentials as a player in the business world. Because of his philanthropic contributions in the aftermath of the 1906 earthquake, he came to the attention of the head of the Democratic Party and accepted their support in the 1911 mayoral race.

Rolph's initial years as mayor culminated in the astonishing Panama Pacific International Exposition in 1915, bringing worldwide attention to the rebirth of a city which, only fewer than 10 years earlier, had been destroyed. Already a millionaire by providing ships and tugs for ocean towing, which were built in San Francisco and in Oakland by his brother-in-law, Joseph P. Moore, Rolph had a plan to enter the shipbuilding business himself with the impending involvement of the United States in World War I. He formed the Rolph Shipbuilding Company in 1917 and purchased the Bendixsen shipyards in Humboldt, California.

In February 1918, he went to Washington, D.C. to meet with the U.S. Shipping Board for the necessary approval to build wooden ships for the French government. That year, he also announced his candidacy for governor of California. By now, he had changed his political affiliation to Republican and, although he was endorsed by the Democratic Party, by law he had to have been endorsed by his own party first. The Republican Party had endorsed William D. Stephens, the incumbent for reelection. Stephens won with 56.28 percent of the vote; Rolph, running as a Republican, received 2.99 of the votes as a write-in candidate.

At the same time, the U.S. Shipping Board, under the Democratic administration of President Wilson, retracted their authorization for Rolph to build ships for the French government, and would not permit him to sell the ships to any other countries for diplomatic reasons.

Rolph returned to Washington to protest the decision, which he claimed was politically motivated, but his appeal was unsuccessful. When World War I ended in November 1918, Rolph was left with no opportunity to recoup the significant investments he had made in this venture, and he was faced with growing debt.

At the same time Rolph was suffering major financial difficulties, China Mail Steamship Lines, founded in 1915 with a ship purchased with the assistance of Mayor Rolph, was financially successful. The board, led by Lew Hing as Chairman of China Mail Steamships Lines, believed that business could increase if it had another ship.

Lew Hing, likely deferring to Rolph's expertise, consulted with Rolph about finding a ship to buy.

"Mayor Rolph, thank you for taking time from your busy schedule to see me," Lew Hing said.

Rolph, in the Mayor's office at City Hall, replied, *"Hing, great to see you again. William tells me that Hoover has approved a long-term agreement for the cannery to provide canned goods to Europe. More money for you and me. We should drink to that success. A drink?"*

Lew Hing was pleased to be greeted so heartily. So pleased he thought to himself, *"I'm finally an honorary white man! That's what money can do."* He then responded with his request, *"On behalf of the board of China Mail Steamship Lines, we want to thank you for your involvement in helping find the SS China in 1915. The venture is so successful that the board would like to ask you to find another ship to buy."*

They discussed what China Mail needed, and Rolph, with a twinkle in his eye and dollar signs on his mind, said he would get back with Lew Hing.

A couple of weeks later, Rolph and Lew Hing met again with Look Tin Eli present. Lew Hing introduced Look as the main force behind the "Tourist" Chinatown and now president of the shipping lines.

Mayor Rolph: *"Glad to meet you, Look, Hing is an old friend and any buddy of his is a friend of mine. Listen, great work with Chinatown! A cigar?"* Turning to Hing: *"Hing, I consulted with ship owners throughout the world and all the passenger ships are in use now. If you can wait until the war is over, we might be able to find a suitable ship to buy."*

Look Tin Eli: *"Mr. Mayor, we would like to proceed as quickly as possible. Is there any alternative?"*

Mayor Rolph: *"Look, there is a burned-out wreck nearby in a shipyard in Portland, Oregon that is for sale. I think I can get it for a good price for you and have it towed to my shipyard in Humboldt and immediately start to refurbish it."* Rolph did not reveal to him that his business was in trouble and needed a project to keep afloat.

Back at the office, Lew Hing said: *"Look, the war is almost over and plenty of ships will be available for us so I advise us to wait."*

But Look was anxious to move ahead as quickly as possible and, based on his discussions with the people at Rolph Shipyards, not knowing they were heavily in debt with no projects in the pipeline, was given a low-ball refurbishing figure.

Look Tin Eli reported his study of the cost to refurbish the *SS Congress* and the board, anxious to move forward, then voted to proceed with the purchase.

The (inevitable) cost overruns, totaling two million dollars for the refurbishing, caused financial problems for the steamship line. It also resulted in an internal war between the management and the conservative stockholders, generating a "death list" with the names of Chairman Lew Hing, President Look Tin Eli, General Manager Lee Lok-chai and sixteen other board members.

Burdened with the financial drain from the *SS Congress*, the company needed to boost revenues. So, along with the *SS China* and *SS Nanking*, China Mail purchased the *SS Nile* after the war ended. However, while volume increased, emerging competition caused a slump in both passenger revenue and cargo revenue as fierce cost cutting began. In an attempt to boost revenue, China Mail looked for new routes. However, its efforts were stymied when the U.S. Congress passed the Jones Act, a protectionist law to stimulate the American shipping industry. It only allowed shipping between one American port to another American port by American-owned and American-built ships, crewed by U.S. citizens or permanent residents. While China Mail ships were American built and crewed by U.S. citizens or permanent residents, it was disqualified because ownership was mainly Chinese, who were aliens and, by law, not able to be naturalized.

CHINA MAIL STEAMSHIP LINES FORCED INTO BANKRUPTCY

1923

Struggling to remain profitable, what ultimately sealed the fate of China Mail were violations of the narcotics drug import and export act of 1922, and the unequal treatment of China Mail compared to other shipping lines. Many of the shipping lines smuggled contraband in the United States. If inspectors enforcing the act found prohibited items on board a steamer, special agents of the Treasury Department would investigate the seizure, quiz the crew, captain, officers and others and then make a report to Washington. The penalty was assessed at $25 per ounce found. The company then was required to give a surety bond for the release of the vessel and appeal to the Secretary of the Treasury for remission or mitigation of the fine or penalty assessed.

Due to numerous seizures of cargo from its ships in the Port of San Francisco, along with the imposition of heavy fines, China Mail was forced into bankruptcy, and all the assets were seized by the federal government to pay the fines. The *SS China* and *SS Nanking* were sold at auction, and the *SS Nile was* sold for scrap. Loans from the Canton Bank to China Mail went unpaid and the Chinese stockholders lost their investment.

During the time of the bankruptcy proceedings, there were unconfirmed rumors that while China Mail was heavily fined and its appeals to the Treasury Department for remission or mitigation were always turned down, other shipping lines also caught with contraband were routinely given a "slap on the wrist" and their fines reduced to nearly negligible amounts.

Six years later, the possibility that China Mail was singled out for disparate treatment was borne out when the *San Francisco Examiner* printed an exposé titled:

HEAVY FINES ON SHIP LESS SEEN AS DOPE EVIL REMEDY

Laxity of Government in Exacting Large Penalties
From Vessels Caught Smuggling
Narcotics Blamed for Influx of Drugs.

> *New York, Jan. 24, 1929.* United States Attorney Charles H. Tuttle of New York says he believes the value of the drugs smuggled into the United States in the last year is something between $23,000,000 and $50,000,000. What has happened to the ships that brought that incredible amount of hideous poison into this country, to be dealt out to the men, women and children of America in horrifying amounts? Most of the cases against the ships that were caught smuggling during this past year are still pending and nobody knows just what penalty

the shipowners and the ships' companies will have to pay.... The narcotic drug and export act provides that when a seizure is made on board a steamer, the ship must put up a bond of twice the amount of the penalty assessed before the steamer can clear from port....

Let's see how this law actually works out. On July 14, 1927, 830 tins of narcotics were seized aboard the *President Taft* in the harbor of San Francisco. The narcotics were valued at $29,300.... When the opium was found, a fine of $146,650 was levied against the company, which put up a surety bond of twice the value of the seizure or $213,300. The company appealed to Washington and the fine actually paid by the *President Taft* was not $146,650 but THREE THOUSAND DOLLARS. Something of a comedown, wasn't it?

On July 1, 1926, 197 tins worth $6,500 were found on board the *President Lincoln* in San Francisco Harbor. The fine levied was $32,823. The bond demanded was $65,650. The company appealed to Washington and paid just exactly ONE THOUSAND DOLLARS in the way of a fine....

On March 14,1925, 119 tins were found on the *West Cho-paka*. The fine assessed against the vessel was $19,700. A bond of $39,400 was put up. On appeal the company paid a fine of FIVE HUNDRED DOLLARS....

The China Mail line, for some reason or other, was not so lucky. OWNERS BANKRUPT. Heavy fines were plastered on the China Mail ships, due to record seizures in the port of San Francisco, and

> the China Mail line was forced into bankruptcy because of these fines… Is there any way of controlling the ship-smuggling end of the "dope" trade? From the history of the China Mail Steamship Company and the present situation in San Francisco, it seems as if there is a very plain, simple and utterly feasible way. How will it be worked out?? Let us watch these particular cases and see.[50]

CONSPIRACY TO CLOSE ETHNIC BANKS

California in the end of the nineteenth century and early twentieth century continued to be concerned with the immigration of people from Asia and the migration of Blacks from the South in search of jobs away from the discrimination and violence of white supremacists. Laws such as the Chinese Exclusion Act in 1882, the Alien Land Act of 1913, and the 1917 Asiatic Barred Zone slowed down the immigration of colored people—but what could be done to drive away those already in California? One way was to strangle their economic development opportunities.

To meet the economic demands of a growing state, banks proliferated in an atmosphere of non-regulation, leading to mismanagement and embezzlement of depositors' money. Regulation was needed as the outstanding problem facing banks was the severe shortage of management talent, particularly for small banks which had restricted investment opportunities.

This problem was coupled with official venality and misappropriation of funds, which proved another recurrent problem. The pervasive incompetence of most bank officials,

---

[50] *San Francisco Examiner*, January 25, 1929.

blurring the line between incompetence and venality in practice, led the legislature to pass the 1910 Banking Law in California.

For minority communities, access to loans from capital white-owned and -operated banks was not available to immigrants or merchants of color for a variety of reasons, but mainly because of racism and discrimination.

For this reason, Black-, Japanese- and Chinese-owned banks were established. However, based on the failure rate of banks formed in Asian communities from 1900 to 1910, the white community was not above using the law to stifle growth of Asian communities, particularly Japanese and Chinese. After this time, no state-chartered Chinese bank was established until 1962 when Cathay Bank was chartered.

In the absence of access to capital by western (white) banks, Japanese and Chinese used rotating credit associations named *"Tanomoshi"* and *"Hui"* respectively, to provide loans to their communities. The Japanese banks were engaged principally in extending credit to Japanese merchants and farmers. However, the Japanese immigrants were somewhat less dependent on Tanomoshi, as the Yokahama Bank of Japan was willing to underwrite their loans on practically no collateral.

The Chinese, with no support from overseas, were thought to finance themselves from their own resources. Prior to the formation of the Canton Bank, *Hui* was essentially the way immigrants loaned money to each other. A form of banking in China, this was traditionally a group of close friends or relatives who had gotten together and put money into the pot.

When the earthquake caused the Russo-Asiatic bank to close, Look Poon Shan and Isaac Allen, executives with the bank, were out of a job. Allen suggested to Look that he start a Chinese bank serving the Chinese community. Look Poon Shan likely shared his idea of a Chinese bank with his brother, Look Tin Eli, who at this time was chosen by Lew Hing to lead an effort to create a "Tourist" Chinatown. At the time, Look Tin Eli, the secretary of the newly formed Chinatown Chamber of Commerce, met with Lew Hing to discuss how to present the idea of a bank to the merchant members.

The timing was right. The merchants needed to fill the stores along Dupont Street so that the "tourist" street could be full of colorful businesses for the whites. A bank was the easiest way to centralize the *Hui* system in light of the overwhelming need to speedily rebuild Chinatown, which is why a bank made sense. This is how a presentation was made to the merchants:

1. In order to establish a bank, the minimum capital needed is $300,000 U.S.;
2. An investor in the bank shall be a member of the Chamber;
3. An investor shall be able to borrow from the bank at a preferred interest rate;
4. An investor may invite any other merchant to apply for a loan but the investor is responsible for repayment of the loan if the merchant defaults on the loan;
5. Any merchant who brings in depositors shall be able to borrow up to 50 percent of the amount of the deposits that collectively, the depositors keep in the bank for at least one year.

Look Tin Eli made a presentation to the merchant members of the Chamber in 1907. After raising more than the minimum required capital, they passed a resolution authorizing the application for a charter to open a bank.

When the bank was chartered and open for business, the Board members included Look Poon Shan, Lew Hing, Lew Hing Gang and Look Tin Eli. Look Poon Shan was hired as General Manager and Isaac Allen as Assistant Manager. For Lew Hing, having experienced the difficulty of accessing capital, he could use the bank system to fund bigger projects. That was the goal of a bank for him, and the prestige of being associated with a bank, albeit a Chinese bank, would give him greater gravitas in the white world.

The advent of the new banking law likely made the Canton Bank operating procedure, a hybrid of the Hui and western banking models, illegal, and this may have caused Look Poon Shan to leave the bank in 1913 for fear of being prosecuted for violating the law.

Elbert W. Davis, in his article "Liquidation of the Canton Bank", compares Asian- and Black-owned banks.

> "In evaluating the contribution of rotating credit to Oriental commerce, it is helpful to compare this informal financial system with more rationalized operations such as banks. Banks provided an obvious alternative to rotating credit associations in that the financial services actually provided by rotating credit associations might alternatively be provided by banks. Most students would simply assume that rationalized financial institutions would provide a more efficient and satisfactory financial structure than an old-fashioned money pool. This premise leads to the corollary supposition that Chinese and Japanese small businesses would have been better served had the Orientals been more active in banking and less active in Hui and Tanomoshi.
>
> "But the dismal histories of Oriental- and Negro-owned banks offer little support for such a view.

> Both Negroes and Orientals opened banks of their own in the first third of this century. The Negro banks and their problems have received substantial attention; Chinese and Japanese banks have not. The experience of Orientals in banking is of considerable importance for the interpretation of Negro banking history since it suggests a standard of comparison. This standard permits the assessment of the relative success that Blacks attained in banking as well as an evaluation of the advantages and disadvantages of banking and of rotating credit as alternative types of lending institutions…."[51]

Regarding bank failures, the author compares the closing of 92 percent of Negro banks, 134 to 11, then continues:

> "Discouraging though this record was, Negro banks in this period were actually more successful than Oriental banks in California, among which the mortality rate was 100 percent. Japanese and Chinese opened ten state-chartered banks in California between 1900 and 1910. Of this number, six closed before the decade was out, victims of the California Banking Act of 1910. One bank survived until 1912, and three others limped along until the mid-1920s.
>
> Characteristically, Japanese banking was more decentralized than was Chinese. The Chinese opened only one bank; the remaining nine were all opened by Japanese residents of California. However, the Chinese-Americans' Canton Bank was substantially larger than any of the more numerous

---

[51] See Elbert W. Davis, *"Liquidation of the Canton Bank,"* California State Banking Department Bulletin 2 (January 1928).

> Japanese institutions and also was longer-lived. In 1920, the California Superintendent of Banks reported the net assets of the Canton Bank as $4.2 million, whereas in the same year, the assets of the two surviving Japanese banks totaled only $1.3 million. Foreign exchange constituted the bulk of the Canton Bank's business, at least in the later years…. When the Canton Bank was suspended in 1926, the Bank of Fresno and the Nippon Bank had already expired. These failures put an end to prewar efforts of California Orientals to operate banking institutions on their own account.[52]

In *Business and Welfare Among Chinese, Japanese and Blacks,* author Ivan H. Light wrote the following:

> "This unhappy record of persistent bank failure offers little preliminary ground for supposing that these institutions were dependable sources of credit for personal or commercial purposes. But the causes of these repetitious bank failures are also instructive. The causes were not random. The banks established by these immigrant minorities were plagued by recurrent problems that tended to systematically bring down the institutions. These recurrent difficulties are of considerable analytical importance, because the rotating credit associations 'happened' to be immune to them. This immunity from the problems characteristically afflicting formal banking institutions suggests the advantageousness of rotating credit as a financial system for the small commercial purposes of these immigrants….

[52] Ibid., Davis.

> "According to the California state superintendent of banks, the single most frequent cause of Oriental bank suspensions was mismanagement. Seven of the ten Oriental banks were suspended at one time or another, and one (the Nippon Bank) was suspended three times before being finally liquidated….
>
> "These problems of administration did not, however, affect rotating credit, Hui and Ko did not require the services of educated, technically skilled administrators. Indeed there were no paid officials at all in the rotating credit associations. The "administration" of Hui or Ko amounted only to opening sealed bids and announcing the results. Since the collected funds simply rotated among the members, tellers did not have to manage the funds. Hence, the problem of financial expertise which recurrently dogged Oriental and the Negro efforts in formal banking did not affect the Oriental rotating credit associations. Lack of technically-skilled officials became a problem only when these poor immigrants attempted to operate a Western-style bank."[53]

In 1913, California attempted to stop Japanese immigrants from establishing a permanent presence in California by passing the Alien Land Act. Japanese banks likely helped finance the purchase of land and, to work around the Alien Land Act, the purchases were in the names of their children born in the United States, such a typical example in the farming community in Florin, California, where one young girl

[53] Light, Ivan H., *Business and Welfare Among Chinese, Japanese and Blacks,* (University of California Press Berkeley, Los Angeles, California; University of California Press, Ltd. London, England, 1972).

had property in her name. (Japanese farmers, however, often purchased land which no white farmer was capable of making productive.)

Using "mismanagement" as a way to close down Japanese banks was an easy proposition for the whites even though the Japanese had abandoned the "Tanomochi" or rotating credit system to adhere to the new banking regulations. After all, there was no threat from Japan in such a minor matter where it did not directly affect trade between Japan and America.

Given the anti-Asian sentiment, first as to the Chinese and then in 1913, the California Alien Land Act "prohibiting aliens ineligible for citizenship" from owning agricultural land or possessing long-term leases (directed at Chinese, Japanese, Indian and Korean immigrants), is it far-fetched to assume that the 1910 Banking Law was part of a plan to stifle business development in minority communities to drive minorities out of California? The failure of 92 percent of the Negro banks and the 100 percent failure of Oriental banks is hard to dismiss.

CANTON BANK ON THE WATCH LIST

The State of California's attempts to drive away minorities by stifling access to capital took a different route for each of the growing minority populations. In shutting down the Negro banks, it was using the method succinctly described by Ivan Light in *Business and Welfare Among Chinese, Japanese, and Blacks*. Referring to closing down Oriental banks, he cited different circumstances for Japanese banks from the only Chinese bank but offered no conclusive underlying reason for the closure of the Canton Bank. He suggests that the closing of Negro and Japanese banks was due to their size and the inexperience and technical incompetence of their bank officials.

However, the Canton Bank, with $4.3 million in assets, was sufficiently capitalized and had competent procedures put in place from the inception by Look Poon Shan and Isaac Allen, the first general and assistant-general managers. Therefore, closing down the bank on spurious grounds of "mismanagement" presented a different challenge for the bank regulators. Also, the regulators were wary of intervention by China as it had done when San Francisco attempted to move Chinatown to the outskirts after the earthquake.

The first time the regulators might have been able to close down the bank was in 1912 when Lew Hing awoke to the news that the Canton Bank and Look Tin Eli were involved in a major opium bust.

The *San Francisco Call* newspaper reported in its front page headlines, "CANTON BANK'S OPIUM SEIZED AS CONTRABAND." The article reported that the California Board of Pharmacy had suspected bank president Look Tin Eli of illicit trade in opium for many years, and when officers attached to the Board of Pharmacy opened a vault in a bonded warehouse, they found 300 tins of opium. Without providing the basis for its assertion, the article went on to say that the Board of Pharmacy was certain that the Chinese bank president and probably the institution itself were members of the "opium ring." The article stated that "this organization, which is said to consist of wealthy Chinese, is reputed to derive an immense revenue from speculation in the contraband drug…" and that "The vault was built especially for the storage of opium, the agents say; and if their information is correct, has housed more than $1,000,000 worth of the drug."[54]

[54] *San Francisco Call*, April 11,1912.

Given the anti-Chinese sentiment, Lew Hing was not surprised at the attention paid by the state Board of Pharmacy to target the Chinese—the question was how to avoid being directly implicated. The California Board of Pharmacy could only seize the contraband goods—it had no authority to shut down the bank. This incident inflamed the whites' perception of the Chinese as a vile race by hinting that the Chinese establishment was implicated in a major disgusting practice—enticing innocent white women through opium dens to be seduced and violated by Chinese. Lew Hing knew from then on the bank had to strictly adhere to the guidelines of the 1910 Banking Law.

CANTON BANK IN TROUBLE

1923

For several years, The Canton Bank seemed to operate without trouble. However, beginning in 1917, the bank, which had extended loans for the Wah Muck operations in Mexicali (Pacific Coast Cannery and Hop Wo Chong) faced possible default of those loans. It began when the U.S. suddenly ended the hunt for Pancho Villa as the United States was drawn into World War I, and General Pershing assumed head of the expeditionary forces in Europe in 1917, less than a year after the hunt for Villa began. The U.S. withdrawal caused financial problems for not only the operations in Mexicali but for Hop Wo Chong and Pacific Coast Cannery, which had been supplying merchandise and food for the Chinese workers and the U.S. troops.

Compounding the problem was the struggle with labor shortages experienced by the cotton plantation (Jick San Yuen) in Mexico. They no longer had access to cheap labor, which was key in competing successfully with American growers across the border. By January 1919, Lew Hing and

Lew Chock Suey traveled to Mexicali to assess the situation. An excerpt from an article by Alejandra Cuellar sums up the history:

> "Initially, Mexico welcomed Chinese migrants who began working the land by planting cotton, a crop so highly valued it became known as "white gold".
>
> "However, nationalist sentiment grew alongside the Mexican Revolution—a radical transformation of Mexican society that championed agrarian reform. Anti-Chinese sentiment festered….
>
> "Xenophobia spread through the northern states of Sinaloa, Sonora and Baja California, culminating in the infamous Torreon massacre from May 11-13, 1911. Forces under the command of the revolutionary Francisco Madero murdered 300 Chinese and tortured hundreds more. Out of fear, many took refuge in the basements of La Chinesca, (Mexicali) an underground network that families used to protect themselves from the blisteringly high temperatures of the desert."[55]

In June 1919, a report from the Mexican consulate at Yuma, Arizona was sent to the immigration department in Los Angeles stating that the Mexicans were unhappy because the Chinese controlled the mercantile and farming interests in Baja California. Some residents of the state felt that governor Esteban Cantu was catering to the Chinese population. It was said that many Mexican citizens opposed the large Chinese immigration into their country.

---

[55] Alejandra Cuellar, *Why a Chinese community settled in the Mexican desert*, October 27, 2018. dialogo chino.net.

On April 17, 1920, Lew Hing received a copy of a very poorly-written letter by one "Charles Chu" alleging that both the Canton Bank and the China Mail Steamship Lines were involved in immigration fraud, claiming that laborers legally entitled to travel overland from San Francisco to Calexico/Mexicali were going to be illegally resmuggled (sic) by automobiles back into the United States.

San Francisco 17th April, 1920
Commissioner of Immigration
Washington, D.C.

Sir,
I have the honour to inform you that the presidents of China Mail S.S. Co. and Canton Bank of this city wishes to bring about two thousand Chinese laborers into Mexicali B. C. Mexico and then resmuggle them into this country by automobile. Now it is about two hundred just arrived here by *S.S. Nile* and China they are continuously to bring them over because they charged more than thousand dollars per head. The manager of Wah Chong of Mexicali, his name called Jim Peter look after the other end because he has a pass to come over Calexico of U.S.A. at any time.

Ng Xing in Calexico as the interpreter.

Yours Faithfully,
Charles Chu

Lew Hing was baffled by this letter. To him, this was a fabricated attempt to smear both the bank and the steamship lines. In fact, since 1912, Southern Pacific had an arrangement with the Colorado River Land Company to bring Chinese labor on its ships of the Pacific Steamship Line from Hong Kong to San Francisco, where they were transferred to its railroad to Mexicali. China Mail had been substituted for Pacific Steamship Lines when Southern Pacific closed down its shipping service.

However, upon receipt of this letter in Washington, the U.S. Secretary of State sent a memorandum asking the district director in San Francisco to request that the Mexican *charge d'affairs* refuse granting the permit to cross into Mexico. If the government had simply contacted Southern Pacific, it could have dismissed the letter's claims as without merit.

By 1921, just several months after the allegation by Chu, the U.S. government specifically prohibited all overland transit of Chinese laborers from San Francisco to Calexico/Mexicali. At this time, the province had a new governor who, responding to complaints that the Chinese laborers were taking job opportunities from Mexicans, complained to the U.S. This action dramatically reduced the number of Chinese in the Mexicali area, affecting the investment interests of Lew Hing. He became worried about the Mexicali operation, in which he had invested a great deal of his money and personally guaranteed loans by another bank to Wah Muck, taking from his own personal fortune to cover the loans.

In 1923, the Chinatown in Mexicali mysteriously burned down and Lew Hing made the decision to rebuild the store, trying to rescue his investment

By March 5, 1926, it was clear to Lew Hing that Wah Muck Trading was in serious trouble, and he asked National Bank in Calexico to make arrangements for him to be able to cross into Mexico.

On May 21, 1926, Lew Hing received two telegrams:

CALEXICO CAL MAY 21 1926
LEW HING
CARE PACIFIC COAST CANNING CO OAKLAND CAL
COMPANY NEEDS ELEVEN THOUSAND THIS MORNING STOP SAY WILL DEPOSIT FIVE THOUSAND THIS AFTERNOON STOP CANNOT GET COOPERATION REGARDING ACCOUNT CAN YOU REMIT BY WIRE
FIRST NATIONAL BANK

CALEXICO, CALIFORNIA 100 PM May 21, 1926
LEW HING
CARE PACIFIC COAST CANNING CO 12 AND PINE ST. OAKLAND CALIF OVERDRAWN SIX THOUSAND LEONARD WONT TAKE NOTE. PLEASE WIRE IMMEDIATELY OR COME IN ANSWER
CHINESE MEX MERC CO 121 P

Lew Hing and Lew Chock Suey went down to Mexicali sometime immediately after to relay the news that both the plantation and store would be closed.

What started so promisingly for Lew Hing with the Rolphs ended up with him holding the bag when the U.S. government had no need for the relationship and the Mayor was nowhere in sight.

On November 6, 1926, Lew Hing received the following letter from the Bank of California:

Mr. Lew Hing
Care of Hop Wo Chong Company
718 Grant Avenue
San Francisco, California

Dear Sir:

Will you kindly call at the desk at your earliest convenience in connection with notes of Chinese-Mexican Mercantile Company on which you are guarantor.

Yours very truly

THE BANK OF CALIFORNIA, N.A.
F. W. Walpy, Assistant Cashier

DEATH KNELL FOR CANTON BANK

The Canton Bank's financial problems, which started with the 1923 bankruptcy of China Mail Steamship Lines and the government's seizure of all the assets alleging non-payment of penalties and fines, severely affected the bank's solvency. Then, the closure of the Mexicali operations compounded the loss of loans made by the bank. Lew himself, feeling an obligation to cover the losses, may have used funds from the Pacific Coast Cannery to cover some of the losses.

On October 10, 1924, Lew Hing received the following letter,

October 10, 1924
Canton Bank
San Francisco, Calif.
Office of the President

Gentlemen:

It being the purpose of certain stockholders of the Pacific Coast Canning Company, Oakland, to institute suit against the Company for an accounting, as well as to place the matter of certain irregularities appearing in the books of the corporation before the office of the Attorney General, I would ask that you advise me whether or not, in dealing with this company, you ever received a copy of an amendment to the By-Laws permitting the President, Lew Hing, to draw against the Company's account without the counter signature of the Secretary.

Section 4, Article 8, and Article 9, of the By-Laws prescribe the mode of issuing checks against Company funds, but it appears that these provisions have never been followed, in consequence of which Company funds have been on a large scale diverted into private ventures of some of the directors without entries being made in the corporation's cash book and ledger. My clients challenge this procedure, and it is with a view to effecting co-operation with and between the Company's banks that I direct your attention to the foregoing.

I have carefully inspected the engrossed minutes of the Company, but find nothing whatsoever covering an amendment to the By-laws relieving the Secretary of the obligation to countersign all checks. Many of the checks run into thousands of dollars in single instances with no entry whatever made in the Company's books of account.

Asking that you give the foregoing your preferred attention with a view to effecting a measure of protection for the interests of the stockholders, I remain,

Yours very truly,
Twain Michelsen

TM/W"

Lew Hing spent the next two hours with his attorney, W. A. Richardson who said the following:

"Hing, the most important line in this letter is the line 'as well as to place the matter of certain irregularities appearing in the books of the corporation before the Attorney General.' Unless the government was already involved, no attorney would include such a statement for fear of being sanctioned by the court for posing a threat.' I think the government is going after you. I can't tell whether it is for any criminal conduct."

Lew Hing went home to think about his next move. He had built an empire the Chinese way but thought he had achieved racial equality in the white world. He thought so long as the whites saw green, there was no problem. He didn't reckon that white men had no tolerance for uppity people of color.

Lew Hing, in pursuing his dream to successfully compete with the whites, didn't reckon on both the government and his competitors joining forces to make an example of him as a Chinaman reaching too far into the white man's territory.

His fatal mistake was twofold: first, the 1918 records showed the Pacific Coast Cannery doing a $2,000,000 annual business, with a financial return to stockholders. The dividend payments were equal to the price of the stock purchased. It was a tremendous stock to own. The problem was the stock was available on the open market and any stockholder was entitled to see the by-laws of an open stock company. Second, Canton Bank was the company's bank, which in turn allowed for the bank records to be open for inspection.

It was the opening that the government was looking for to bring down Lew Hing and the Canton Bank. Like the takedown of Al Capone, the government looked for a weak spot. The difference is that the State of California didn't want to put Lew Hing in jail, only destroy him financially, to send a message to any Chinese that, no matter how smart and accomplished, they could be shut down.

He told his attorney to delay Michelsen as long as possible, as he knew that a smoking gun lay in the bank documents. Because it was an immigrant bank and many of the borrowers likely did not have sufficient collateral to secure a loan, money was loaned in a manner similar to the old Chinese *Hui* or revolving credit method.

There was no stopping the government. Attempting to not alarm the public, the Superintendent of Banks began its investigation quietly. However, in the tight-knit community of the 100,000 mostly-Chinese depositors of the bank in the United States and Mexico, word leaked out, causing a run on the cash and forcing the closure. The Superintendent claimed the investigation revealed substantial irregular practices and the bank was ordered closed for good in July 1926, citing "mismanagement". Interestingly, no charges of embezzlement or official venality were alleged against Lew Hing.

Today, nearly a century later, financial redlining by white banks continues, and to aid recent immigrants from China, *Hui* still exist for those who lack American credit and employment history, or are maybe undocumented, to access capital they can't otherwise get from Western banks. But *Hui*, those rotating credit associations, have their own problems. In New York in 2017, two *Hui* worth a combined $22 million collapsed. Here's an interesting note on that event:

> "John Chan, a fixture in Brooklyn's Sunset Park, was consulted when the *Hui* collapsed. He acknowledged that *Hui* failures have created problems even he can't solve, despite his sway with local politicians and law enforcement. But he points out that they've also transformed his neighborhood. Chan walks down to Eighth Avenue, which is lined

by a mile-long strip of Chinese-owned businesses. He says via a translator, "Ten years ago, nobody would even walk down this street, now you can't even buy real estate here."[56]

THE CROWN JEWEL LOSES ITS LUSTER

China Mail Steamship Lines had been forced into bankruptcy in 1923 and the assets seized by the government; the Mexican businesses were losing money hand over fist and needed to be closed; the government had placed the Canton Bank in receivership and was likely to close it down; and Lew Hing was personally liable for guarantees on more of his ventures than he cared to count. To rectify the situation, to pay the debts and hopefully save his business reputation, he would have to sell the crown jewel, Pacific Coast Canning Company, at a huge loss.

As he sat alone in his darkened office at the cannery, he contemplated the end of his business empire. The only thing left would be Hop Wo Lung, the little dry goods store at 718 Grant Avenue—that's where he would be receiving his mail in the future. The hotels, the import/export stores, the other businesses he invested in—he would move to sell his interests in all of them.

But the most painful to lose would be the Pacific Coast Cannery Company. One of the reasons Lew Hing sought to invest in businesses where either he would have an edge over the Chinese competition or avoid directly competing with white competitors was the knowledge that the whites could easily shut him out of the market. Despite attempts to create

---

[56] Ryan Kailath, *Immigrant Lending clubs provide capital, at a cost.* 2017. 90.5 WESA radio.

a seemingly white-owned cannery, he could not avoid being shut out by the competition in the end.

In 1916, the California Fruit Canners Association (CFCA) had consolidated its business with three other large canners to create California Packing Corporation ("Calpak"). Using the Del Monte brand to take center stage, the new company's strategy was to offer one high-quality brand, advertise it nationally and distribute products nationally. The other canneries included Griffin and Skelley and the Central California Canneries Company. At the time of its organization, Calpak had a combined operation of sixty canneries.

By 1917, Calpak became the first U.S. fruit and vegetable processor to advertise nationally, with the first Del Monte brand advertisement appearing in *The Saturday Evening Post*. In 1920, Calpak established the Del Monte guarantee, stringent specifications for its premium brand, Del Monte. Early ads assured customers "Not a label, but a guarantee."

Without a network and advertising budget, Lew Hing had had to find a new market, and that market was Europe. The Buckskin brand had become popular because of Hoover's relief efforts in Belgium and, after the war, in other parts of Europe. Ultimately, 75 percent of the products were sold in Europe, ceding the U.S. market to the white canners.

Lew Hing's efforts to diversify away from reliance on the cannery eventually had found him preoccupied with a multitude of businesses, so many that he could not devote as much time to the cannery as he had done in the beginning. As a consequence, the goose that laid the golden egg back in 1905 was old now and he could do little but watch as a threat to his cannery's profitability was challenged by the whites. The competition wanted nothing more than to eliminate a strong competitor. Unfortunately, Lew Hing's last-ditch plan to form a group of Chinese-run canneries to challenge the hold of the Calpak cartel fell victim to the conspiracy to take down Lew Hing.

The most prominent of the casualties among the group of Chinese-run canneries was the one owned and operated by Chew Sai Yen. The father of Thomas Foon Chew, later to be known as the Asparagus King, Chew Sai Yen operated a small cannery known as Presidio Cannery (mistakenly called Precita Cannery). It had leased space and use of equipment from a white-owned cannery located on Sansome Street prior to the 1906 earthquake. With the cannery operation terminated by the destruction of the property, Chew Sai Yen turned to Lew Hing, whom he knew as a fellow clansman in the Four Family Association, for assistance in starting up a new operation. In 1908, the new Bayside cannery in Alviso opened with Lew Hing as President, Chew Sai Yen as Vice President and Thomas Foon Chew as Foreman. Lew Hing, as with other businesses, was simply a figurehead, perhaps having arranged credit not through Canton Bank but through Mu Tin.

When the son, Thomas Foon Chew, inherited the cannery upon his father's passing, he increased the size of its operations to include plants in Alviso, Isleton and Mayfield. The son was both innovative and forward looking. He incorporated many new technologies along with modern equipment and improved working conditions. Commodities canned at the Alviso plant included spinach, asparagus, cherries, apricots, plums, peaches, pears, tomatoes, catsup, tomato sauce, hot sauce, tomato puree, fish sauce, fruits for salads, vegetables for salad and later fruit cocktail.

His Isleton plant, built in 1919, canned spinach and asparagus. In 1921 they began canning green asparagus, and Thomas Foon Chew became known as the Asparagus King because of his many new techniques to improve and maintain quality.

Bayside rose to become the third largest in the United States after Del Monte and Libby. The death of Thomas Foon Chew in 1931, and the impacts of the Great Depression, effectively ended the enterprise and it closed for good in 1936, perhaps also a victim of the whites' successful attempt to marginalize competing minority businesses.

Lew Hing sat in the dark office of the cannery, contemplating his fate. Both he and James Rolph were now past their prime and the world was fast passing them by. Rolph still was pushing on but his personal finances, like Lew Hing's, were a mess. The time when Lew Hing had been of value to Rolph was long gone—and vice versa.

His Cuban cigar dimly illuminated the room. There was still money coming in from various illicit activities but it barely filled one shelf of the vast space within the vault. In fact, it only filled up four suitcases, placed by the door for a quick getaway.

Lew Hing reviewed his options. Under heavy scrutiny, he knew he had to be careful to not draw too much attention. He knew that he would be found responsible for the amount that was missing from the cannery accounts. He could use the illicit funds to pay back the account, but then he would have to explain the source. The only way to cure the deficit was to sell the cannery outright or find a merger arrangement.

Lew Hing turned the desk lamp on, read the document on the desk in front of him one more time, sighed, and signed his name at the bottom of the following document:

> San Francisco, Calif., May 3, 1926
>
> In consideration of Ten Dollars ($10.00) cash, receipt of which is hereby acknowledged, we hereby give to H.E. Rusk an option to purchase within

> thirty days (30) all of our canning plant, or plants, real estate and machinery, belonging to the Pacific Coast Cannery Company for the sum of Four Hundred Thousand Dollars ($400,000) and Four Hundred Thousand Dollars in preferred stock in the new corporation that will be formed to take over the business of the Pacific Coast Canning Company, it being further agreed that the Four Hundred Thousand Dollars ($400,000) (in part) cash will be paid within sixty days (60 days) after the formation of the new corporation.
>
> PACIFIC COAST CANNING COMPANY
> By President

On June 4, 1926, National Packing Corp., with plants in Ogden and Provo, merged with Herbert Packing company of San Jose, CA and Pacific Coast Canning Company of Oakland to form the Pacific Coast Canners, Inc.[57]

Pacific Coast Canners, Inc. was incorporated in Utah on August 9, 1926. The Ogden plant was operated by Pacific Coast Canners from 1926 to 1932. The Provo plant was operated by Pacific Coast Canners from 1926 to 1938.

"Pacific Coast Canners was a canning company in the western United States. Evidence exists for the company existing as early as 1928; a Trustee's Sale report noted that the company had been registered in California, had land in Alameda and Santa Clara Counties, and was having its Ogden property sold at auction."[58]

A newspaper article about incorrectly weighted lug boxes suggests that Pacific Coast Canners had a plant in

---

[57] *Oakland Tribune*, June 4, 1926 (Source: Utahrails.net)

[58] From vasonabranch.com

Oakland in 1930. Boxes shrank by weight when dried, cutting the money given to growers.

The company suffered a strike in 1935 *(Oakland Tribune, March 31, 1935)* and the Oakland cannery burned down in a fire on July 6, 1938. *(July 6, 1938 Bend Bulletin)*

NINE

GONE AND FORGOTTEN
1926 - 1934

LEW HING
5/1858 - 3/1934

JAMES ROLPH
8/1869 - 6/1934

Lew Hing and Sunny Jim Rolph died within four months of each other in 1934. They are, if anything, a footnote in history; one known as the first Chinese-American industrialist and the other, the longest-serving mayor of San Francisco.

Sunny Jim Rolph died during the third year of his first term as governor of California. Rolph's success as mayor of San Francisco did not carry over when he moved to the Capitol and was confronted with the enormous challenges that accompanied the Depression years. His personal popularity suffered when he refused to pardon Tom Mooney[59] in 1931, and the final blow was his infamous approval of the 1933 mob lynching of the two men held responsible for the kidnap and murder of a well-known San Jose businessman. At the beginning of 1934, Rolph suffered a stroke as he began his campaign for the next term; he was kept at Saint Francis Hospital for a month, but did not recover and soon afterward announced that he would not continue his campaign. He went to recuperate at the Riverside Ranch in Santa Clara, owned by his friend Walter Linforth, and died there on June 2, 1934. The people of San Francisco turned out in the rain by the thousands to pay tribute to Mayor Rolph in City Hall for the last time.

Gov. James Rolph, c. 1930s

It was likely that Rolph was too ill to pay his respects to Lew Hing or perhaps he had forgotten him and of course, Lew Hing was not at City Hall to pay his respects to Rolph.

AN ATTEMPT TO RISE BACK UP

Lew Hing never quit trying to clear his name. To do that, he needed to pay off all his debts. He had negotiated cash from the sale of Pacific Coast Cannery; the cash undoubtedly

[59] Thomas Joseph Mooney was an American political activist and labor leader who was convicted with Warren K. Billings for the "San Francisco Preparedness Day Bombing" of 1916. Governor Rolph refused to pardon Mooney. *Oakland Tribune*, Volume 116, No. 112, 21 April 1932.

came from his ownership of the land upon which the cannery stood. He would draw on this dwindling resource to settle the family accounts.

He felt a fatherly duty to provide for his family and, while paternal instinct likely drove this desire, he was foolish enough to believe they would be grateful.

Lew Hing, c. 1930s

Lew Hing was in a financially perilous position, not only paying the gambling debts, covering the opium and brothel habits of his sons, he was also covering the debts of the Mexican venture, the Bayside sardine cannery, the hotels and import/export stores and other failed ventures of his sons.

He could no longer rely on the thousands previously gained from illicit activities as before. The government had cracked down on the opium trade through laws on importation and use, so only gambling remained as a major revenue generator—but not like the old days. He would use the gambling revenue to support his children and their families.

He took one last stab at the cannery business. On June 4, 1928, he assumed a lease from Lew Wing for a fractional portion of a cannery owned by R. Hickmott Canning Company. It was a joint venture between the two, in which Lew Wing and his associates would contribute $10,000 and Lew Hing would contribute $20,000 to install machinery and equipment to pack fruit. Lew Hing organized a corporation named West Shore Packing Company, which was the assignee of the lease.

The West Shore Cannery took over the processing of fruit from the Pacific Coast Canners of Oakland and continued operations until the U.S. government, in 1931, confiscated all its assets, allegedly because it was somehow connected to Lew Hing.

PART TWO

CHINATOWN AS SANCTUARY

1930s TO 1960s

RACISM ALIVE AND WELL IN AMERICA

1930s

By 1929, when the Great Depression began, the whites had achieved their goal of subjugating the Chinese. According to the U.S. national census, in 1880, there were 105,465 Chinese in the United States, then 89,863 by 1900 and 61,639 by 1920. During this time, Chinese immigrants were placed under a tremendous amount of government scrutiny and often denied entry into the country on any possible grounds.

Unlike Ellis Island, Angel Island immigration station was established in 1910 not to welcome Chinese immigrants but to find a reason to deny them entry. "Initially, customs service officers individually and arbitrarily administered exclusion. In time, procedures became standardized and as they did, exclusion enforcement eventually fell upon the Bureau of Immigration, forerunner of today's Bureau of U.S. Citizenship and Immigration Services (USCIS), formerly Immigration and Naturalization Service. By the first decade of the 20th century, a national system had formed for specifically regulating Asian immigration." [60] Under the continuing anti-Chinese pressure from white society, Chinatowns were established in urban cities, where the Chinese could retreat into their own cultural and social colonies. It was here that the Chinese could find sanctuary from the violence by whites.

For my grandparents and father and mother, San Francisco and Oakland Chinatowns represented the only places they felt safe. The next two and a half generations of my family's existence, from the 1930s to 2000, were defined by life in the Chinatown bubble.

---

[60] *Enforcement: The Question soon arose of how to actually implement the Chinese Exclusion Act*, Angel Island Immigration Foundation, aiisf.org.

EXISTING IN THE CONFINES OF CHINATOWN

1934

When Lew Hing died in 1934, he was, according to my father, a broken man, his business empire crushed, by what my father said was extreme prejudice by whites. My father told me: "I was sixteen when he died and I remember him coming to our house to discuss matters with my parents. Sometimes, over meals, he would start cursing the actions of the whites who he thought were his friends and those he knew were his enemies, ones who would not defend him and the others who thought him too successful for a Chinese and whom they blamed for employing white women and so needed to be taught a lesson."

Bruce Quan and son
Bruce Quan, Jr., c. 1990

This response to my question over lunch with my father in the 1990s opened a window into the past: "We have Lew Hing reunions celebrating his life and accomplishments," I said to him, "but no one talks about why, if he was so successful, what happened to end it all?"

Like many Chinese in America in the 1950s and 1960s, my parents did not speak about family matters and admonished my brother and me to never speak about anything related to our family. "Silence is Golden" we were told. This was because of the Communist scare of the McCarthy era, which "…forced Chinese not to take a stand on anything…It forced them to be silent and unwilling to speak out."[61]

In 1991, I had arranged a weekly lunch with my father. We ate every week at the same restaurant in Oakland Chinatown on the same day, at the same time, both having our same meal for nearly a decade—some 500-plus lunches. It was my idea to break down the wall of silence, and to let my father share the stories of my family.

Our discussions represented a treasure trove of oral history of the life of my great grandfathers, Lew Hing and Quan Ying Nung, my grandparents Quan Yeen and Lew Yuet-yung, and my father and mother. Of the many stories he shared, I have grouped those in which my family's lives were touched or altered by the tenor of the times, and the overwhelming influence of racial prejudice, and share them here in this book.

I asked my father, "What was it like for you growing up?" He replied:

"The 1920s were a period of anti-Chinese prejudice. We had to be very careful outside the house. Because we lived in a white neighborhood, I remember none of the white kids would play with me. I was very lonely and the white teachers were very abusive towards me. I told my father about the teachers and he said, 'This is their world. They never wanted us here so there is nothing we can do. You need to remain silent, no matter how angry you become.' Then he told me what I told you when you complained about being treated badly, 'When you are in the presence of white people, you always look down, never in their eyes. If they address you,

---

[61] Ryan Kim, "Keeping Tabs On Chinatown / Premiering documentary shows how Red Scare cast pall of suspicion on an entire community", *San Francisco Chronicle,* March 10, 2001

you always answer 'No sir or yes sir.' You never talk back or challenge what they say.' "

Chagrined, I said, "Why did you behave like this and tell me to do the same?"

He responded, "When I was young, I asked your grandfather the same question and he said in San Francisco in the late 1890s through the 1920s, everyone knew the true stories of the random murders of Chinese men. Chinese weren't allowed outside of the immediate Chinatown area except if they worked as a cook or houseboy for white families. If the

Lew Hing residence on Lake Merritt, Oakland, at 457 Stowe Avenue, built in 1911.

police found someone Chinese who didn't belong in the white areas, they would take him to the cliffs where the land met the ocean and practice shooting. When the man was dead, they would carry him to the rocks and throw him into the ocean. It was a warning to Chinese to stay where they belonged."

I asked my father, "If the Chinese were separated from the whites and only allowed to live in Chinatown, why did we grow up and live in the white area?" He answered:

"Because Lew Hing's Pacific Coast Cannery was the largest employer in Oakland in the early 1900s, the white politicians allowed him to build a house on the shores of Lake Merritt in 1911. As the cannery grew into one of the most prominent businesses by 1917, he was able to purchase homes for his children in the Jewish area around Grand Avenue and Lakeshore Avenue, starting with your grandfather and grandmother in 1921."

"Were there problems with us being in the white areas?"

"No, because your grandfather was involved with the underworld activities in San Francisco and Oakland, of which the whites in power partook. In addition, their police were well compensated to look the other way. In fact, up until 1935, your grandfather was deputized as an Alameda County Sheriff, allowed to carry a gun."

"Did you encounter much racial prejudice as a child?"

"There were incidents of racial prejudice but only when I interacted with whites outside of Chinatown. Because my entire childhood, even through college, was spent in the Chinese community, interactions with whites were few and far between. Even at public school, except for grammar school which was nearly all white, there were enough Chinese in junior high and high school and at Cal for us to socialize among ourselves."

At the time, because of the hostility of the whites towards Chinese, our family's cultural and social activities were one hundred percent within the Chinese community; mainly Loong Kong (family association) and CACA, (Chinese American Citizens Alliance) both headquartered in San

Francisco and Oakland Chinatowns. Of course, we were expected to marry within the race. But, even if one wanted to marry outside the race, as you did, there were anti-miscegenation laws in place."

A LIFE ALTERED BY RACIAL PREJUDICE 1940-1965

Chinese Students at UC-Berkeley, 1940. The author's father, Bruce Quan, is second from left, top row.

My Dad was the first in our family to attend college. When he graduated from Oakland High School in 1936, he enrolled at U.C. Berkeley that Fall. At the time, U.C. was socially segregated and the Chinese mostly shunned. As a result, Phi Alpha Phi fraternity, of which he was a member, had been established by Chinese students. Similarly, Sigma Omicron Phi sorority was established for Chinese women students for the same reason. The Chinese also formed a social club, having been largely excluded from other mainstream social groups.

My father majored in Electrical Engineering at Cal and met my mother, Anna Choy, in 1939 at the Golden Gate International Exposition at Treasure Island in San Francisco where she worked as a concessionaire's employee.

Bruce Quan and Anna Choy, marriage photo, 1942

In 1942, my parents went to Reno to marry. His parents had disapproved of their marriage and had forbidden him to marry my mother because she was not Sam Yup but Sze Yup. In addition, her father was a lowly candy shop owner in Crockett, California. As a result, my grandparents initially disowned my parents, refusing to help financially. Without support, my father left Cal before graduating. My mother told me that this incident led to bitterness between him and his parents until they died.

"What happened after you and Mom married?" I asked.

"We had financial problems but fortunately, there was a shortage of electricians working in the shipyards and my electrical engineering professor at Cal was able to get me into the local union, IBEW 595. My pay barely covered the rent and other expenses. Also, your Mom was unable to find a job although she had just graduated from secretarial school at Armstrong College. All the Chinese businesses told her they didn't need a person with her skills and white businesses told her they didn't hire Orientals. Finally, we moved to San Francisco where Chinese nightclubs were hiring and because I was big and tall for Chinese, I had a second job as a bouncer at night."

RACIAL PREJUDICE IN THE SERVICE 1942

In 1942, my father waited to be drafted. While he waited, he joined the California Militia, formed shortly after Japan bombed Pearl Harbor. According to one history, "Chinese American men in both Los Angeles and San Francisco demonstrated their patriotism by voluntarily forming special companies for the California Militia. There is no documentation of these efforts in military records—except for an insignia used by the Los Angeles Chinatown militia as part of its insignia—but a few photographs and personal reflections attest to the existence of these military units."[62]

Bruce Quan marching on Grant Avenue with Chinatown unit of the California State Militia.

[62] Dresser, Norine, *California Militia and National Guard Unit Histories*, Chinatown Militia Units 1942, Los Angeles and San Francisco, Military Museum.org/Chinatown Militia Units.

My father told me, "The whites couldn't tell Chinese from Japanese so we were the target of racial slurs. When both your Mom and I took the train or bus, we carried a sign around our neck saying "I am Chinese." So when the California State Militia formed a special unit for the Chinese, I joined and, having been in ROTC in high school and at Cal, I was given an officer-rank position. I thought it was a good way to demonstrate patriotism to the whites."

My father was working at Moore Drydock in Oakland from 1942 until he was drafted in early 1944. While at Moore, the union refused to promote him from Apprentice to Journeyman although he was more than qualified. The first child, my brother Melvin, was born in February 1944 and by May of that year, my father ended up at Fort Lewis in Seattle, Washington. According to him, it was a living hell as he endured racial taunts and had to fight whites who attacked him in the off-hours while living in the barracks. He was finally able to secure off-base living and sent for my mother and my brother.

THE INCIDENT IN NEW ORLEANS WHILE AT OFFICER CANDIDATE SCHOOL

1945

My father was proud of his military service. He had saved many pictures of himself in his ROTC uniform at Oakland High and Cal, in the Chinatown Unit of the State Militia, as an enlisted serviceman and, after serving in World War II, as a Captain in the Army Reserves for another twenty years.

Now, years later, I was curious about his military career. One day at lunch, I asked, "What was it like being in the South during the war?"

"It was okay." This was his standard response, but this time I pressed. "Did you experience racism in Louisiana while you were at Officer Candidate School?" After further prodding, my father eventually opened up with a long monologue.

Bruce Quan in the U.S. Army

"It was 1945 and our class had just completed training. We were given weekend passes to go into New Orleans. Two buddies—both white—and I went together in uniform."

He paused to slurp some soup, wiping his mouth before returning to his narrative. I was struck by how clearly he recalled details, as though it had happened yesterday,

"I needed to go to the bathroom, and we eventually found one in a department store. As I neared the bathroom, I suddenly stopped. When my buddies asked why, I pointed to the sign over the door: *Whites Only*. Another sign said *Colored* with an arrow pointing to the back of the building.

One of my buddies said, 'Colored means Negroes,' and besides, you're with us so it's okay.'

"We went in. As I stood at the urinal, a white civilian came in, spotted me, and said in a loud voice, 'What the fuck is he doing in here? Yellow bastards like him belong in the back with the niggers'.

"It took all my willpower to not respond. But one of my buddies showed no such restraint. He did to the man what I wanted to do, confronting him and knocking him out.

'That'll teach the fucker to mess with the U.S. Army,' my buddy said, grinning.

"I was gratified that they'd come to my defense, but the incident shook me. I kept thinking, what if I'd been alone?"

DREAMS AND AMBITIONS THWARTED 1946

Discharged in 1946 with a second son on the way, my father looked for work. He first went to the union but they refused to promote him from the apprentice program as they didn't want the stain of a minority member sullying the all-white membership. So he ventured out on his own, hoping to parlay his education, work experience and military service into a good paying job.

"I was discharged in 1946, the year you were born, and had a family to feed. The economy was booming and jobs were plentiful. Because the union refused to promote me, I applied for job after job but was rejected at every turn. Rejections were sometimes accompanied by outrageous comments, 'We don't hire Japs so why would we hire Chinks?', 'Why would we hire a Chink when so many white veterans are available?' and 'Why don't you go back to where you came from and find a job? We don't want your kind here'."

For the first time I understood how my father's ambitions and dreams had been thoroughly thwarted by racism. A victim of injustice, he had vented his frustration on his children. And while my brother took it stoically, I fought back. That caused our estrangement for years after I left home, a week after graduation from high school.

RACISM ON FULL DISPLAY

1952

After opening the door on a discussion of how racism affected my father, I sensed he felt more at ease speaking about racism, so over lunch, I asked, "Dad, do you remember any racial incidents happening to our family when Mel and I were young?"

He paused to think and then responded, "One day, you, Mel, Mom and I were going to a family association dinner in San Francisco Chinatown. You were about six. There were no parking spaces on the Chinatown side of Broadway as since the end of the war, the population in Chinatown exploded with returning Chinese veterans, their war brides and children. Parking was impossible. I saw some on the North Beach side but I didn't want to park there because there had been several racial incidents involving the Italians reported in Chinatown. After circling for half an hour, Mom said we should take our chances and park on that side of the street…"

Dad continued to talk but I barely heard him. A memory had taken hold of me. Mom, Mel and I were getting out of the car in our Sunday best…a young tough in a leather jacket with greased-back hair approached us…went for my mom. "Let's see what's under here," he spat, making a motion to reach under her dress.

She clutched my brother and me tightly and backed away against the car.

"Leave my mom alone." I kicked at him but got only air.

My father, now out of the car, ran toward the guy, but just then another man in a black jacket emerged from the shadows and slugged my father on the back, causing him to stumble. As my father clutched the car fender to keep from falling, this new guy spat on him. "What are you going to do about it, Chink? You know better than to park on this side of Broadway. This is North Beach!"

Now five or six other young toughs were standing just a few feet away. Another stepped forward and spat on my father. "Go back to Chinktown," he snarled, pointing to the other side of the street.

In the distance I saw a man in a blue uniform. "Mr. Policeman!" I screamed. "Help!" He glanced in our direction, not moving.

That diversion gave my mother enough time to push us into the back seat of the car, shouting, "Lock the door!"

Mel and I scrambled in and he pushed the lock button down. Mom opened the front door, jumped in, slamming and locking the door.

My father scrambled to his feet, backed his way to the driver's door, and got in.

As he started the car, the one who tried to touch my mother put his face close to the window, causing my mother to recoil. I stared in horror as he pressed his face against the window, licking it and making smacking noises. He grabbed the handle and tried to open the door. "Fuckin' bitch!" he shouted. He stepped back and kicked the door, and was about to do it again when Dad started up and pulled away.

Looking back, I saw the group of white men laughing. I would always remember the cop, a fat white man with a ruddy face and red nose, joining the group, slapping one of the punks on the back and laughing heartily.

Fear and anger shook my body as I sobbed openly, my little fists clenched in tight balls. At the first stoplight, after wiping the spit off my father, my mother reached over and pulled me to the front seat and held me close. My brother lay curled in the corner of the backseat, his coat pulled over his head.

"Hey, Bruce," Dad said, shaking me from my reverie. "Are you okay? You seemed to be in another world."

"Just listening to your story," I said.

Recalling that memory caused my palms to sweat and my breathing to quicken. It was difficult to maintain calm. It was no wonder I had buried that memory deep in my memory bank.

Why did the whites detest the Chinese so much? I thought that China, being allied with the United States in World War II, would have reduced the animosity by whites towards Chinese. But that apparently wasn't the case. The memory of this particular incident recounted by my father caused me to search for a reason why racism against the Chinese continued to thrive.

White racism might have been rekindled by the War Brides Act of 1945. Effective on December 28, 1945, the Act allowed alien spouses, natural children and adopted children of members of the United States Armed forces, "if admissible," to enter the United States as non-quota immigrants after World War II.[63] Exempting spouses and dependents of military personnel from quotas established by the Immigration Act of 1924, the War Brides Act allowed 84,517 women and children to enter the United States until its expiration in December 1948.

Although the Act was promulgated chiefly to benefit the whites in the military (the 1882 Chinese Exclusion Act had been repealed by the Magnuson Act in 1943), Chinese Americans, of any Asian groups, benefited the most from the 1945 law.[64] The Immigration service tried to limit the admission of the Chinese, employing detainment procedures

---

[63] War Brides Act (59 Stat. 659, Act of Dec. 28, 1945)

[64] Zhao Xiaojian, *Remaking Chinese America: Immigration, Family, and Community, 1940-1965,* (2002). Rutgers Press. P. 79

for Chinese wives and children. For example, on January 28, 1947, the *San Francisco Chronicle* carried an article entitled "Captive Vet Brides" criticizing the INS for holding Chinese wives and children of Chinese veterans "incommunicado" or without communication with their families. Similar criticism came from the Chinese community as the January 28th issue of the *China Daily* claimed that 350 Chinese war brides were detained, sometimes up to a week.

Limited by housing restrictions, the returning veterans and their brides could not simply blend into different communities but were forced to live in Chinatowns. The perception of overcrowding in the Chinatowns led whites to assume that the Chinese were once again poised to overrun the United States, rekindling the fear of "yellow peril." In reality, of the 84,517 foreign wives, around 49,000 came from Germany and France. Only 5,132 came from China.[65]

LEGACY OF HATE

1953

My first direct encounter with racism happened when I was seven, in the company of my buddy, Raymond.

"You and Raymond be careful. Don't walk too far down Grand Avenue," Mom said as we were leaving out the door. "Yeah, yeah," we echoed in unison as we ran down the front steps that sunny summer day in 1953.

Walking past the Grand Lake Theatre, the cigar shop, the diner and Kosher butcher, we made our way to the end

---

[65] Ting, John H., *Intersectionality of Race and Gender: A Story of Transnational Marriage and Chinese "War Brides" in Post-WWII America,* A Honors Thesis, History Department, Rutgers University, April 2010, page V.

of the shopping district where Mandana Street emptied onto Grand Avenue. I had never been beyond this point.

"Let's keep going," I said to Raymond. "Let's explore!"

"Uh, your Mom said not to go too far."

"Oh, come on, like there are no dragons or bad stuff ahead," I said. "Are you chicken?"

We kept walking past houses and an occasional store until I looked up and the street sign said Oakland Avenue.

"Let's turn back," Raymond said, uneasy.

Suddenly, a car traveling in the opposite direction pulled a U-turn and screeched up next to us, scaring both of us. I looked quickly and saw it was a police car. One cop got out and stood over us. He was big and white. As we were taught, we never looked up from the pavement and only responded when asked.

"What are you, Chinks or Japs? And what are you doing here?"

I stuttered, "Chinese. We were just walking down the street."

"You don't belong here," the cop responded.

I heard the car door slam and the other cop got out and stood next to his partner, grinning. I glanced up and saw him reaching for his billy club as his partner put his hand on my back pushing me to bend over. He placed his leather ticket holder on my back and the other hit me with force, sending me sprawling. They then hit Raymond the same way. As we lay on the ground crying, one cop said: "If we ever catch you Chinks here again, it'll be worse!" Then we heard them laughing as the car drove off.

Stunned, we lay there for what seemed like an eternity before slowly picking ourselves up. After the pain subsided, Raymond said, "What was that about?"

Walking back home, I wanted to find out why the policemen did what they did but was also afraid to tell my Mom what happened.

I responded, "I don't know, but I bet that was why my Mom said don't go too far down Grand Avenue.

My mother noticed we were both upset. "What happened?"

Afraid to tell at first, I eventually spoke up, through tears, about the incident.

Chiding us, she said, "Didn't I warn you not to go too far down Grand Avenue?"

That night, I remember, clear as day, asking my mother, "What is a Chink?"

Putting down the book of fairy tales she was reading, she paused and said, "It's a word white people use when they don't know your name."

Puzzled, I ventured, "Then it's okay for me to use it to greet a white schoolmate if I don't know his name?"

She smiled, "No, it's a bad word white people use to describe you and me as Chinese people. They use it when they don't like you. Let's finish the story so you can sleep and be ready for school tomorrow."

Boy, was I confused.

IN THE BELLY OF THE BEAST

1958

For most of the second half of the twentieth century, Oakland, California was a divided city, whether by politics, geography, race, or economics. The affluent hills were all white, thanks to *de facto* segregation, and the flatlands of West and East Oakland were populated by blacks. The Chicanos were in Fruitvale and the Chinese mostly in Chinatown. The flatlands, except for areas around Lake Merritt, housed the economically-challenged minorities next to the polluting industrial businesses owned by the whites who lived in the hills or Piedmont.

As my mother said to me during my near daily visits to her while she was on her deathbed suffering from cancer, “We actually thought that it was okay to live in Montclair as the freeway from there was a quick commute to the U.C. Radiation Laboratory in Berkeley where your Dad had just gotten his first decent paying job.”

Montclair was, with the exception of a very few minorities, all white, and it was well known that real estate agents would not show houses there to non-whites. My parents borrowed money from my aunt, my mother’s sister, and began the search for a home. Every real estate broker marketing homes in the Montclair area refused to show homes to my parents citing the restrictive covenants in the deeds which forbade home ownership to Orientals, along with other minorities. The truth, according to my mother, who spoke with Mrs. Smith, a social worker and our next door neighbor, was the brokers were afraid if they “broke the color line”, they would be branded as traitors to the white race.

In the end, my father had a buddy from his unit in the Army reserves buy the house and then transfer it to my parents. When we moved in during the summer of 1958, the summer months were completely spent fixing up the house. In the fall however, my father, my brother and I were out in the neighborhood daily, going to work or school. Oh, the uproar that ensued when the people in Montclair saw yellow people lived in the neighborhood!

My Dad, perhaps buoyed by the prospects of actually making a decent union wage, took the racism in stride. He would come home from work and recount incidents.

"Driving down Thornhill, a white driver coming in the opposite direct showed me the finger," and he chuckled as he said it. Or, "At the stoplight at Moraga and Thornhill, a white guy yelled, 'Hey, go back to where you came from, you blank blank'." I think my father took satisfaction from violating their comfort zone, knowing they couldn't do anything about it.

My mother had similar encounters with racist white women. Having had much experience with such confrontations, she said she learned to remain calm. I remember her telling me, "A fat white woman came up to me and pointed a finger in my face and said, 'You don't belong here,' to which I calmly responded, 'Why don't you go back to your country since the only people who are natives are the Indians.'"

SEGREGATED SCHOOLS

1958 - 1964

I went to Westlake Junior High in the Fall of 1957. Unlike Lakeview elementary school, which was nearly all white, the students at Westlake fairly reflected the racial composition of Oakland: blacks, browns, whites and yellows. At Westlake, you either were tormented or a tormentor and if you chose the latter, you needed to "gang up." With Chester, Ray, Ignacio, Hook and Don, we were a multi-ethnic gang of sorts. It was at this early age that exposure to kids of a different color helped me to be "colorblind" as I grew up.

Coming together to avoid being bullied, we learned to protect each other. We fought before homeroom, in homeroom, at lunch, and after school. The weapon of choice in school was a car antenna because you could easily snap it off at the base and it telescoped to more than two feet long. It was free and easily replaceable. I didn't have to worry if my shirts or pants were torn in a fight because most of my clothes were hand-me-downs, from our cousin Barry to my brother Mel to me.

I was a "latchkey" kid, essentially without supervision during the day. So instead of going home after school, I would hang out with my gang. We engaged in all sorts of mischief, fighting, stealing, drinking and rolling drunks if we came upon one.

The move to Montclair in 1958 wrenched me from an idyllic beginning in my younger years into a living hell with attendance at the then-segregated Montera Junior High School. Universally ignored by fellow students, I remember only one other Chinese classmate in my class—my lifelong friend Victor Gong. Over the years, we compared notes of racism and discrimination in junior high and high school.

In 1961, I attended newly opened Skyline High School. The school board, wanting to create an all-white school to protect white children from mixing with minorities, drew boundaries designed to avoid areas of families of color. High school was a miserable experience for the few minorities because if you weren't white, you experienced severe social segregation.

I learned the lesson of my place one time early in my high school career. I had looked forward to a dance after school. Entering the gym, I saw it was decorated and I anticipated having a good time. I saw a group of girls with whom I shared some classes, and watched them dance with some boys also in my classes. I took a deep breath and approached the girls.

Nervously, I said, "Would any of you like to dance?"

They all looked at me, there was a silence and then one of them said, "We don't dance with your kind." Then they all turned away as if I wasn't there.

I left embarrassed, then looked back to see they were being escorted to the dance floor by other boys. I went to the door and told the teacher I needed to go to the bathroom. I left the gym, went to sit on the bleachers for the rest of the dance, waiting for my mother to pick me up. I stopped attending school dances and any other school socials.

RACISM IN THE OPEN

FALL 1964

"Hey you, you don't belong here!" The booming voice echoed through the crowded room, silencing the band playing "Louie Louie."

My friend Cliff and I were in the room, standing on the periphery. It was a balmy evening after the first Cal home football game and the electricity of anticipation of raging hormones pulsated in the air.

I was excited—my first year at Cal, a new experience for me. Berkeley was rocking and we had been walking past a fraternity house at the exact moment dozens of young people spilled out into the yard, dancing, drinking and laughing.

"Let's go in," Cliff said. I nodded hesitantly—all white people, I noted—but followed, gently sliding through the crowd. In the dim light of dusk, I thought I detected looks of disdain.

In the aftermath of the shout out, the room fell silent and suddenly the crowd parted as several burly white men approached. One snarled, "You slant-eyed motherfuckers, don't you understand English? Vamoose! Scram! You don't belong here."

We froze at the sight of them and as they pushed us forcefully towards the exit, the crowd egged them on, hatred etched on their faces. I heard snickering and someone yelled, "Yeah, get those yellow bastards out of here."

"Those fucking assholes," I said to Cliff once we were outside, my temper unleashed. "I wish we could have duked it out."

"Bruce, calm down. With those odds, you would have had ten of them all over you before you threw the first punch."

I was still seething as we walked down Bancroft to Kip's, the campus burger joint. I kicked at a parking meter in frustration.

"Bruce, let it go," Cliff said gently. "We've been through this before. You can't change them."

Although the racism of the whites was something I had experienced directly on many occasions, at that instant, I felt crystalize inside me an understanding of why my parents had assiduously warned me about whites. I had endured both silent and overt racism at the segregated high school I attended, getting the message after being turned down asking white girls to date or dance. Although I developed some friendships with fellow students, I was never invited to join any of them in social activities outside of school; my social life consisted of dating Chinese girls from other high schools in Oakland.

By the time we walked into Kip's, I was distracted but no longer fuming. Turning to Cliff, I said, "I now understand why my parents called them 'Lo Fann'—white devils."

PART THREE

UNDERCURRENTS OF RACISM REMAIN

CIVIL RIGHTS MOVEMENT

1965

My attending Cal coincided with the Free Speech Movement in the Fall of 1964 and the Civil Rights Movement that had been challenging racial discrimination against blacks since the early 1950s. It was a time of optimism, where attempts to right past wrongs were made. Congress passed landmark anti-discrimination laws, first the Civil Rights Act of 1964, then the Voting Rights Act of 1965 and finally the Fair Housing Act of 1968.[66]

Exposed for the first time at Cal through participation in marches and demonstrations in support of freedom of political speech on campus, civil rights and against the "immoral war", I rejected the safety of the conservative subculture of the Chinese-American community and looked for a new identity. Leaving the university to find myself in 1967, I worked in a paint factory for a year with salt-of-the-earth black Americans who had left the South to escape extreme racism. Returning in the fall of 1968 with a new perspective on how deeply racism had permeated every corner of society, I became involved in the founding of the Ethnic Studies Program in 1970 and later taught or worked in the administration of Asian American Studies, Afro American Studies and

[66] The Civil Rights Act of 1964 explicitly banned all discrimination based on race, color, religion, sex, or national origin in employment practices, ended unequal application of voter registration requirements, and prohibited racial segregation in schools, at the workplace, and in public accommodations. In 1965, the Voting Rights Act restored and protected voting rights for minorities by authorizing federal oversight of registration and elections in areas with historic under-representation of minorities as voters. And in 1968, the Fair Housing Act banned discrimination in the sale or rental of housing.

Native American Studies. I graduated with three undergraduate degrees in Zoology, Sociology and Asian American Studies, the latter being the most important degree, as my thesis for the degree was the History of Asians in California. Through the research, I was stunned to learn about the enduring racial hatred of Chinese and later Asians by whites in power from the time of the arrival of my ancestors in San Francisco to the present day.

Passing legislation to ban discrimination is one thing—overcoming the implicit bias in all walks of life, from education to business to government, is another. So, upon graduating from Cal in 1971, I enrolled at the Berkeley Law School to fight for equality of opportunity and social justice.

RESPONDING TO RACISM

1975

While in law school, the focus of social justice took the form of advocating for equality for all citizens or residents regardless of race, gender or national origin. There, in my first year, I participated in a strike for more student input into the diversification of the entering classes through the admission process. In the second year, I was student body president at Cal, leading an effort to expand the

Growing old in the ASUC

By ASUC President Bruce Quan

From the 1973 UC Berkeley "Blue and Gold" yearbook

Pell Grant program to state colleges and community colleges where more minority students attending college needed financial aid. In my third year, I worked for the Senate Watergate Committee investigating misuse of power by President Nixon.

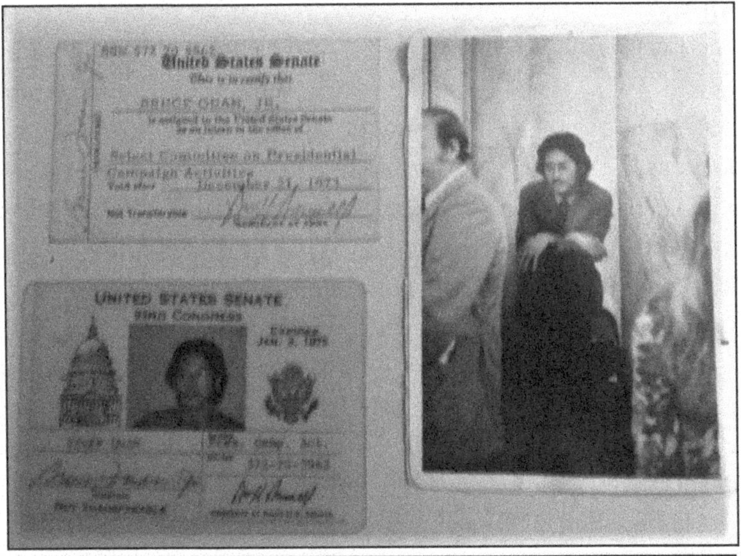

Bruce Quan, Jr., credentials for Senate Watergate Committee.

Graduating a year late because of my work in Washington, D.C., I participated in the interviewing process with employers in the Spring of 1975. I had heard from my classmates who had graduated earlier that a large numbers of minority applicants were uniformly rejected by law firms. I had a job offer already but was curious as to why law firms avoided hiring minorities.

I interviewed with several high-powered law firms from the major cities—New York, Washington, San Francisco and Los Angeles. Almost immediately, rejection letters filled my mailbox. But one spring afternoon, I struck gold.

I met the recruiter from a major law firm in New York, a mid-level associate. He spent time reviewing my resumé and letters of recommendation, after which he took a deep breath and exclaimed excitedly, "What was it like working for the Watergate Committee and what were your responsibilities?"

I was happy to talk about it. "When I started in the summer of 1973, I was assigned to the Watergate Break-in and Cover-Up group, first tracing the money that ended up in the pockets of the burglars. Then with the revelation of the taping system in the oval office, our unit became the litigation unit, and I researched and drafted the first pleadings for the presidential tapes lawsuit. Thereafter, I drafted the immunity orders and pleadings for the defense of the Committee against the lawsuits filed by Nixon partisans. The next summer, Chief Counsel Sam Dash asked me to draft the final report of the activities of the Watergate Break-in and Cover up section."

He replied, "You come with stellar recommendations from those you worked for on the Committee and, but for you being a minority, we would hire you in a heartbeat. I have to tell you that despite your qualifications, we don't hire women or minorities."

At last, someone who let down his guard. So I said, "I'm curious as to why your firm has this policy?"

"Well, two reasons. The first is that sometimes we meet with clients and need to have an associate in the meeting. We have found that some clients feel uncomfortable with someone who might not look like their son. And second, partners have stated that hiring minorities or women might mean our firm was unable to attract talented white males and it might cause prospective clients to question the quality of our work."

I thanked him and immediately went to see Marty Africa who was in charge of the Cal placement office. I recounted my meeting with the interviewer and she thanked me for the information.

Again, you can legislate against discrimination but you cannot force those in positions of power to change their racist attitudes overnight.

RACISM IN PRACTICE

1978 - 1984

It was 1978 and I left the Alameda City Attorney's office to enter private practice.

Wanting to engage in trial practice, I held myself out as a litigator. One day, in a faraway county in California, I had arrived early for a hearing in the county courthouse. Upon checking in with the court clerk at the assigned courtroom, she excused herself and went back through a door. Returning, she motioned to me to follow her.

She ushered me into the judge's chambers where he was sitting behind the desk. He looked me up and down and then said, "What are you doing here?"

I replied, "My name is Bruce Quan and I am the counsel for the plaintiff, your honor."

"I know that. I mean what are *you* doing here?"

"I don't understand, your honor."

"You don't belong here."

I was stunned and at a loss for words. He then waved his hand to dismiss me.

I waited outside the courthouse and when my client showed up, I explained the situation. I told him to leave and went back into court. I asked for a continuance because my client was ill. I recommended the client find a white attorney to represent him.

In sharing my experiences with minorities who went into court, we all had stories of those early days, when most of the judges were white men. As a minority attorney, you were sometimes "hometowned" in your own county, which meant that if you were in court in a different county, say Fresno, the judge would give the opposing, local (Fresno) attorney an advantage in rulings. Minority lawyers were sometimes subjected to being "hometowned" in our *own* county by white judges where the opposing counsel was a white male.

Those years, 1978 to 1984, were lean years. The Chinese wanted white attorneys to represent them, afraid of being at unfair advantage if I represented them, and the whites had their own attorneys. So, I temporarily left the practice to start an import/export business. When the import/export business began to flag, I took a position with the federal government as a senior trial attorney and then with a local redevelopment agency as assistant general counsel. It was then that I realized why Chinese attorneys in the 1950s and 1960s either worked in the government or became immigration attorneys—the white law firms would not hire them.

I was lucky as by the early 1980s, China was opening up and I was able to find clients interested in doing business with China. That led to my involvement with the San Francisco Shanghai Sister City Committee, which brought additional clients.

Eventually, my practice involved representing Chinese companies doing business in the United States and American companies doing business in China. I had enough business that in 2000, I left behind the struggles against racism within the domestic legal system for Beijing where I stayed until retirement in 2013.

I am heartened by the increasing diversity of the judicial branch, both federal and state, but there is still a major imbalance between the majority of white males versus women and minorities on the bench.

RACIAL PROFILING IS ALIVE AND WELL

1989

A quarter of a century after the groundbreaking passage of the Civil Rights Act, white institutional racism remains alive and well in America.

When I was young, I thought all those racial slights and incidents were my fault—that I somehow wasn't a real American. In my lifetime, progress has been made toward racial equality, but something always happened to remind me that racism was still alive and well in America.

In 1989, as the interim city attorney of the City of Alameda, I was the chief legal officer of the city. One night, after an unusually late City Council meeting, I returned to my office upstairs in City Hall to prepare instructions for the secretary. It was nearing 2:00 am.

Leaving the darkened City Hall, I drove past police headquarters onto Lincoln and then to Park Street headed towards Oakland. A block later, a police car pulled up behind me with its sirens blaring and lights flashing. I pulled over and rolled down my window.

The police officer immediately left his car and walked over to my car door, and in a harsh tone said, "Get out of the car, boy, and spread them." I reluctantly got out and leaned over, putting my hands on the hood as I was told—very perturbed.

"Show me your license," he said, "carefully," as I stood up and reached towards my back right pants pocket.

I gave him my license and he said, "Get back on the hood." I glanced back and saw him looking at it with his flashlight. At the time, I lived in Berkeley and maybe his tone was because of this fact.

Then he said, not at all courteously, "Boy, what are you doing here at this hour? You don't belong here, you belong on the other side of the bridge."

By this time, I was furious and, not wanting to speak while upset, held my tongue.

He repeated his question, this time in an accusatory tone, "I asked you, boy, what are you doing here?"

Moments passed before I responded, "Officer, I am your City Attorney."

There was a dead pause and then I heard him mutter under his breath, "Oh shit." Then, the bullshit started to flow from his mouth, "I really apologize for this mistake. I'm sorry to have stopped you but, you know, we have a report of an Oriental male committing a robbery."

"Can I get off my car and have my license back," I said, still upset.

"Yes sir, yes sir," he said as I turned to face him; leaning in close to his face, I said, "You mean, you have a description of an Oriental male wearing a business suit driving a red sports car?"

He stood silent, knowing I had caught him in a lie.

He looked away as I continued, "Officer, you know racial profiling is cause for disciplinary action? I need your name and badge number. I'm going to have a talk with Chief Bob in the morning."

"Oh, sir, it was an honest mistake, please don't report me to the chief."

The next morning, still pissed off, I walked to my office, two doors down from the Mayor's office. Through the open door, I saw the Mayor and he waved me in. Closing the door behind me I began, "Chuck, you have a problem," after which I described the incident. He slammed his hand on the desk and said he would talk to Chief Shiells. I gave him the information on the offending cop and said, "If you have higher political aspirations, you need to address this problem."

Some time later, after I left the city attorney position, I remember hearing a news item on the radio about the Alameda police having been caught on tape denigrating African Americans, calling them, among other things, "monkeys" and "jungle bunnies."

After the initial furor, I heard no more about the incident. I didn't follow it up, guessing it had been swept under the rug like many similar racial incidents involving the police.

The incident rekindled many memories of my growing up Chinese in America and often hearing my grandfather's warnings to me.

"Be careful, little one," YeYe would say.

"Be careful of what, YeYe?"

"When you are away from the house, be careful of the Lo Faan (White Devils)."

"Who are these White Devils? How will I know one?"

YeYe, trowel in hand, was down on one knee patting the dirt around a rose bush. Stopping, he looked at me and said, "The Luk Yee (police) are all Lo Faan. They beat and shoot Chinese for no reason. You must be careful where you go. When I was young in San Francisco, if the Luk Yee found a Chinese person in the wrong part of the city at night, they would take him out to where the ocean was, use him for target practice and after killing him, toss the body into the ocean."

What YeYe said confused and troubled me. "Why do they do this?"

"Because they hate us," he said, patting the dirt into a mound.

His admonitions had long been banished to the recesses of my mind—that is, until I read *Driven Out*, by Jean Pfalzer. The author documented the ethnic cleansing of the Chinese in cities and towns of the western United States in the 1870s and 1880s. The book brought back more details of my talks with him.

Grandfather's lessons focused on the need to be docile, submissive, and self-effacing. "Make sure you lower your head as you speak…make use of 'yes sir' and 'yes ma'am'. White people like that. It makes them feel superior…" He chuckled, "…even if they speak only one language while we speak two."

It eventually occurred to me that Chinese people born in America had become adept at modifying their behavior to conform to white-defined standards. It was why we became known as the "Model Minority." Of course, it was necessary to survive in the white world.

CORONAVIRUS: WHAT ATTACKS ON ASIANS REVEAL ABOUT AMERICAN IDENTITY

2020

From the BBC News, 27 May 2020, Helier Cheung, Zhaoyin Feng and Boar Deng

Attacks on East Asian People living in the U.S. have shot up during the pandemic, revealing an uncomfortable truth about American identity.

Though she was not born in the U.S., nothing about Tracy Wen Liu's life in the country felt "un-American". Ms. Liu went to football games, watched "Sex in the City" and volunteered at food banks.

Before the Covid-19 pandemic, the 31-year-old didn't think anything of being East Asian and living in Austin, Texas. "Honestly, I didn't really think I stood out a lot," she says.

That has changed. With the outbreak of the pandemic that has killed around 100,000 people in the U.S., being Asian can make you a target—and many, including Ms. Liu, have felt it.

In her case, she says a Korean friend was pushed and yelled at by several people in a grocery store, and then asked to leave, simply because she was Asian and wore a mask.

In states including New York, California, and Texas, East Asians have been spat on, punched or kicked, and in one case even stabbed.

Whether they have been faced with outright violence, bullying or more insidious forms of social or political abuse, a spike in anti-Asian prejudice has left many Asians, which in the U.S. refers to people of East or Southeast Asian descent, wondering where they fit in American society.

"When I came here five years ago, my goal was to adapt to American culture as soon as possible," says Ms. Liu.

"Then the pandemic made me realize that because I am Asian and because of how I look or where I was born, I could never become one of them."

After her friend's supermarket altercation, she decided to get her first gun.

"I hope the world never comes to a day when we have to use that, " she says, adding: "That would be a very, very bad situation, something I don't even want to imagine....".

POSTSCRIPT

The seeds for scapegoating the Chinese in California first appeared in the 1860s. Whereas in the 1850s the early Chinese immigrants had been admired for their industry and frugality, by the 1860s the Chinese were considered to be "an inferior race" and a "degraded" people. By the 1870s, the racist argument had broadened in scope, and the Chinese were viewed as "a social, moral and political curse to the community."

Variations of the following arguments against the Chinese are still used today to justify attitudes towards minorities.

- **The economic argument**, as advocated by nativist and workingmen's groups, that cheap Chinese labor undermines wage rates and adversely affect employment practices on the West Coast;
- **The cultural argument**, that the once-enlightened Chinese civilization is now corrupt and backward, and that Chinese immigrants represent the lowest classes in China;
- **The assimilationist argument**, that the Chinese do not deserve to merge into the American mainstream and, with their "abounding vices" (prostitution, gambling, opium-smoking) are impervious to the "loftier ideals" of Western civilization;
- **The racist argument**, that America should maintain a homogeneous population and that national degeneration would ultimately result from permitting an inferior race (the Chinese) to mingle with a superior race (the Caucasian);

- **The biological argument**, that the Chinese are "inferior in organic structure, in vital force, and in the constitutional conditions of full development";
- **The medical argument**, that the Chinese, ignoring all laws of hygiene and sanitation, breed and disseminate disease, thereby endangering the welfare of the state and of the nation.[67]

[67] Adapted from Joan B. Trauner, "Chinese as Medical Scapegoats," 1870-1905, *California History Magazine*, 1978.

FAMILY GALLERY

FAMILY GALLERY

These photographs are precious reminders of the Lew and Quan families through the generations.

Great Grandfather Lew Hing and Great Grandmother Chin Shee, c. 1880

Great Grandfather Quan Ying Nung and Great Grandmother Tom Shee, c. 1900

Children of Quan Ying Nung and Tom Shee, c. 1890
L to R: Quan Jan, Quan Yeen, Quan Poon, Quan Jwe

Grandfather/mother Quan Yeen and Lew Yuet-yung, c. early 1900's

Lew Hing with children Thomas and Rose, with Ralph on his lap, at Idora Park, Oakland, 1908.

Lew Hing Family at 457 Stowe Ave., Oakland, 1913; Quan Yeen & Lew Yuet-yung family at far left.

Quan Yeen and Lew Yuet-yung Family, 1924
L to R, back row: Quan Ying Lin's husband, Quan Ying Lin (famous opera star), Ralph Quan, Randolph Quan
L to R, front row: Lew Yuet-yung, Bruce Quan, Quan Yeen

Bruce Quan and
Anna Choy Quan, c. 1950s

Bruce Quan Family, c. 1962. L to R, seated: Anna, Bruce Jr., Bruce holding Ardene; Melvin standing behind Bruce Jr.

Bruce Quan, Jr. at marriage to Jane Zhao, San Francisco, 1996. L to R: Nathan Eckrich (stepson), Bruce Jr., Melvin Quan (brother).

Bruce and Jane driving to Palace of Fine Arts after the wedding, for photographs, 1996

Bruce Quan, Jr. and Jane Quan Family, 2004
L to R: Jane, Noelle, Bruce Jr., Bruce III ("Boo")

Bruce Quan, Jr. and Jane Quan Family, 2012 in Beijing
L to R: Bruce Jr., Bruce III, Noelle, Jane

APPENDIX A

LEW HING BUSINESSES AND INVESTMENTS

Lew Hing Businesses and Investments

Name in English	Name in Chinese	Nature	Year	Place	Investment	Role
			Businesses			
Hing Kee & Co.	興記	tin shop	1874	SF		principal owner
Pacific Fruit Packing Co.	和興記	cannery	1887	SF	$10K, total $50K	Manager
Hop Wo Lung I	合和隆	General merchandise	1895	719 Commercial, SF	$2K, total $30K	partner, Lew Kan manager
Tai Fung Co.	泰豐公司	cannery	1899*	SF	at least $4550	shares held under Liu Man Sing Tong
Fook Heng	福亨	silk and fabrics	1902	Canton, China	￥2K, total cap ￥7500	partner
Wuet Lun Dispensary	活倫	pharmacy	1902	Canton, China		partner
Lai Hing	澧興	finance	1903	Canton, China	1000 taels, total cap 30K taels	partner
Liu Wah Cheung	劉華彰	fabrics/clothing	1903	Canton, China	1500 taels, total cap 12K taels	partner
Heng Tai	恆泰	dried seafood	1903	Hong Kong	HK$500, total HK$8K	partner
Pacific Coast Canning Co.	華安公司	cannery	1904	Oakland, CA	$8000, total cap $50K	President
Unknown		Fruit ranch	1906	Winters, CA		managed by nephew
Republic Hotel	共和旅館	hotel	1907	710 Dupont, SF		partner with Choy family
Canton Bank	金山廣東銀行	bank	1907	SF	$10K? Initial cap $300K	VP/President
Wing Lay Yuen	永利源	lottery	1907	Oakland, CA	Initially $8100, total cap $25K	2nd largest shareholder
Sing Chong	生昌	fancy goods	1907*	601 Dupont, SF		
Fook Loy	福來	lottery	1908	Oakland, CA	Initially $9600, total cap $20K	principal owner
Fook Woh Nanking	福和南京	fancy goods	1908	SF	$6K, total cap $100K	Asst Manager 1910
Mun Ming Hotel	文明旅館	hotel	1909**	868 Clay, SF		parter with Look family
Leung Kwong Minning Co.	兩廣煤鑛公司	mining	1909	Guangdong province	stock public offering X3, 3rd time 5K yuan	Manager 1909
Hop Wo Lung II	合和隆盛記	General merchandise	1910	718 Dupont, SF	$2K (later $3K), total $30K	President
Hong Yan Tong Wing Kee	同仁堂	herbs	1910	315 8th St., Oakland, CA		** in 1908 CSYP new year issue

(Credit: Roland Hui)

Lew Hing Businesses and Investments

Name in English	Name in Chinese	Nature	Year	Place	Investment	Role
China Elite	.	ladies furnished goods	1910*	1011 Washington, Oakland, CA		
Mun Ming Hotel	文明旅館	hotel	1912	868 Clay, SF		parter with Look family
Chinese Mexican Merchantile Co.	華墨商務公司	General merchandise	1913	Mexicali, Mexico	$60K as of 1926, total cap $120K	President
China Mail Steamship Co.	中國郵船有限公司	shipping	1915	SF	$4,200 as of 1916, total cap $2.1M	VP/Board Chairman
Jik Sang Yuen	植生園	cotton plantation	1918	Mexicali, Mexico	$4750 as of 5/1918, total $100K. Later majority owner.	President
Bayside Cannery		cannery	1918	Monterrey, CA	at least $30K loan from Griffth-Durney	
West Coast Improvement Co.			1924		65 out of 500 shares at $100 par	President
West Shore Packing Co.		cannery	1928	Antioch, CA	LH to raise $20K or more, Lew Wing $10K	

* To be confirmed

** Between Oct. 1906 and Sept.1909

Investments

Name in English	Name in Chinese	Nature	Year	Place	Investment	Role
Hang Far Low	杏花樓	restaurant	1880	SF	$100, total $10K	shares held under name Wo Hing Kee
Sun Ning Railroad	新寧鐵路	railroad	1910	Toishan, China	￥500	
Sun Hui Land	廣東商辦岡州公所	real estate	1913	Sun Wui, China	200 taels silver	
Foo Kwan Real Estate Co	福群實業公司	real estate	1914	China	200 "Eagle silver"	
	華粵信託銀行	bank	1917	U.S. East Coast	$1,000, total cap $20K	
Canton Tea Garden	廣東茶園	tea	1922	Chicago, IL	$2000, total $450K	
Honor Manufacturing Co	安亞製藥行	pharmaceutical	1922	Canton, China	￥1100	
Hing Ah Match Co	興亞火柴公司	match manufacturing	1922	Canton, China	$1000 (￥2000)	
Far Eastern Trust & Savings Bank	遠東實業儲蓄銀行	bank	1923	Canton, China	HKD$2000	
Foochow Importing Co	金山福州公司	import co	1923	550 Grant, SF	$300, total cap $21750	
Oriental Commercial Bank	東方商業銀行	bank	1923	Hong Kong	HKD$20K	

APPENDIX B

FAMILY GENEALOGY CHARTS

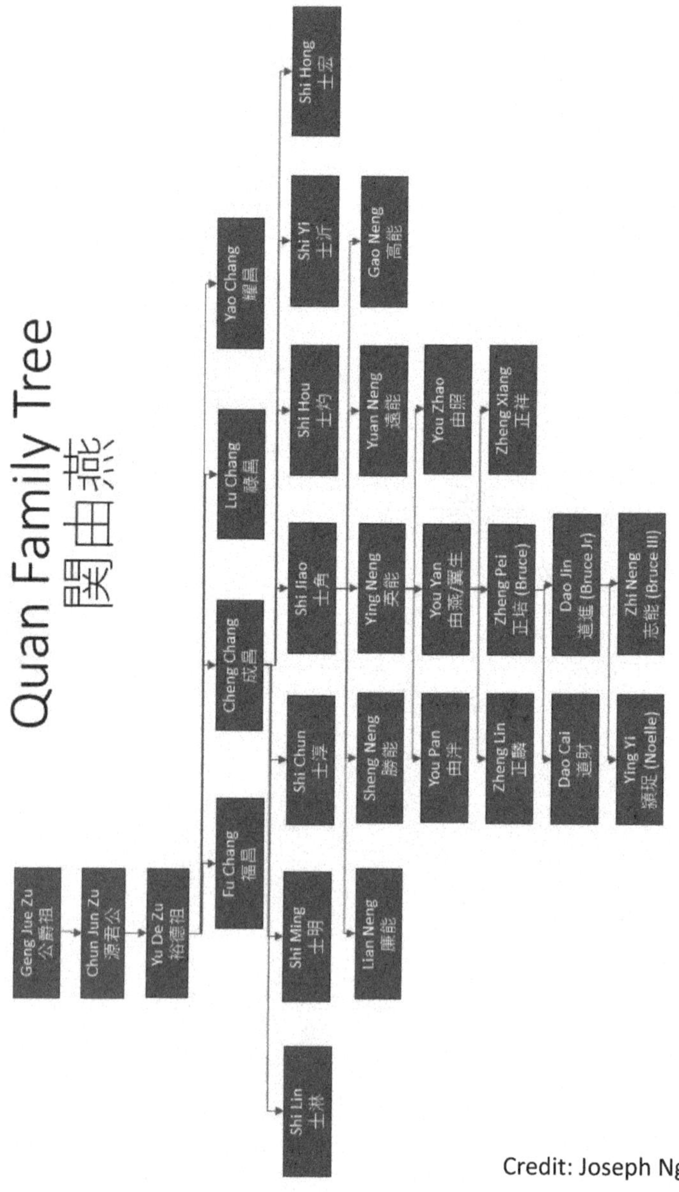

Credit: Joseph Ng

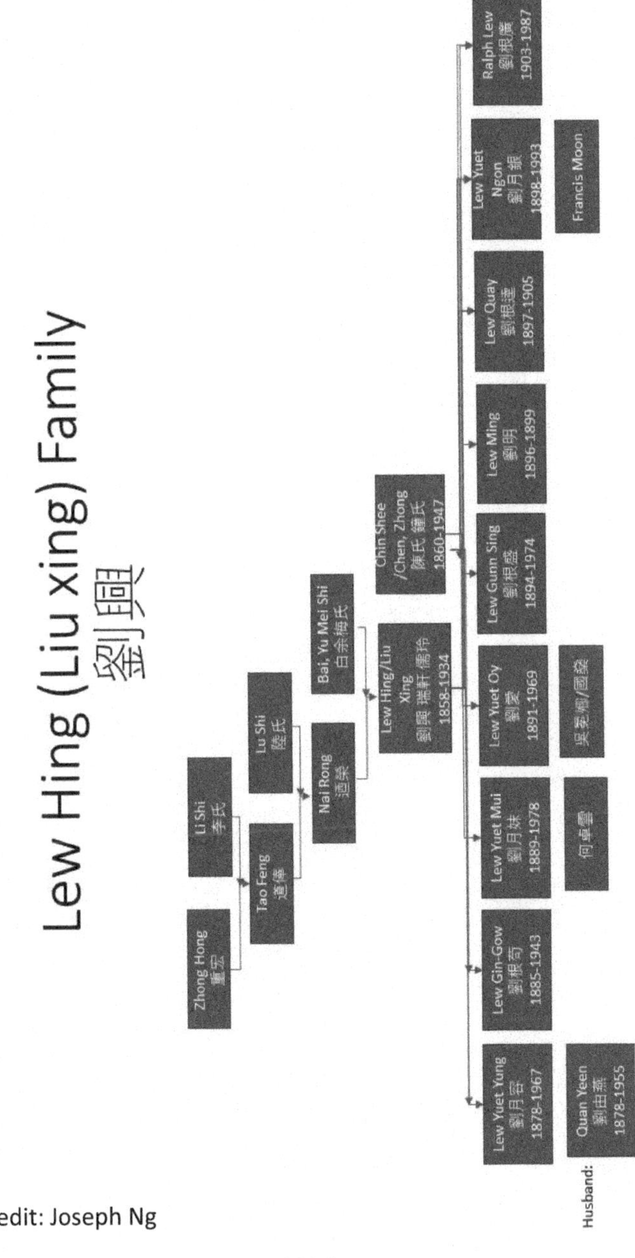

Credit: Joseph Ng

ABOUT THE AUTHOR

Bruce Quan, Jr. is a fifth-generation Californian whose family relocated to Oakland in 1906 after the Great San Francisco Earthquake. He was born in Sacramento in 1946, while his father was serving in the army.

His great grandfather, Lew Hing, founded the Pacific Coast Canning Company in West Oakland in 1905. It was one of the largest employers in Oakland.

Bruce attended Oakland schools, graduating from Skyline and then attending the University of California, Berkeley. He received undergraduate degrees in Zoology, Sociology, and Asian American Studies, and a law degree from the Boalt Hall School of Law (now the Berkeley Law School) in 1975.

While attending Berkeley, he was a community activist for social justice and participated in the Free Speech Movement and the Vietnam Day Committee. Bruce was elected student body president at U.C. in 1972, where he championed environmental awareness, promoted safety on campus for women, and childcare for single mothers. In the late summer of 1973, Bruce was chosen as one of three students nationwide to clerk for the Senate Watergate Committee. He later returned to Washington in the summer of 1974 to draft the Watergate "Cover-up" and "Break-in" sections of the committee's final report.

Upon graduation from law school, he worked in the City Attorney's office in the City of Alameda where he was responsible for environmental, planning and zoning matters. In 1978, he opened a law practice and advised Oakland's Mayor Lionel Wilson on economic development issues in

Chinatown and downtown areas. In 1988 he moved his law practice to San Francisco, and served Mayor Art Agnos as General Counsel for the San Francisco-Shanghai Sister City Committee and the San Francisco-Taipei Sister City Committee. In 1994, Quan ran for a seat on the San Francisco Board of Supervisors. He placed seventh out of 26 candidates contesting for five seats.

In 2000, Bruce moved his family to Beijing and continued his law practice, and worked as a professor with Peking Law School. In 2001, he accepted a senior Of-Counsel position with the international group of Allbright Law Offices, then the largest law firm in China, where he represented Fortune 500 companies doing business in China. While in Beijing, he served for four years as a member of the Board of Trustees of the International School of Beijing (ISB) and as a Vice Chair for the Public Policy Development Committee of the American Chamber of Commerce in Beijing (AmCham).

Since retirement, he has returned to Oakland and re-engaged in issues affecting the Chinese community in which five generations of his family have been involved, and on a wider scale, issues of social justice, public safety and economic development in Oakland.

ACKNOWLEDGEMENTS

I am very grateful for the enthusiastic encouragement I received, while composing this book, from many friends and family members. I would like to also thank Mary Burns for her assistance in editing, designing and publishing *Bitter Roots*; Stu Gardiner for his excellent work on making many of the aging family photographs come to life in these pages; and Cynthia Ciganovich for her proof-reading skills and sharp eye for consistency.

A website is currently under construction. In the interim, to contact the author, please send an email to bruceqj@prodigy.net .

Copies of this book may be purchased on Amazon.com.

Made in USA - Kendallville, IN
1232385_9798682626786
02.12.2021 0829